W9-AVQ-594

KEITH BEASLEY-TOPLIFFE

Surrendering to God

LIVING
THE COVENANT PRAYER

PARACLETE PRESS
Brewster, Massachusetts

Library of Congress Cataloging-in-Publication Data

Beasley-Topliffe, Keith.
  Surrendering to God : living the Covenant prayer / by Keith Beasley-Topliffe.
    p. cm.
Includes bibliographical references.
   ISBN 1-55725-284-X (Frenchfold)
1. Prayer. I. Title.
  BV210.2 .B36 2001
  248.3'2—dc21   2001004099

10 9 8 7 6 5 4 3 2 1

Published by Paraclete Press
Brewster, Massachusetts
www.paracletepress.com
Printed in the United States of America.

Contents

Acknowledgments

THERE ARE MANY PEOPLE I would like to thank for their help in the creation of this book. Evelyn Newman greatly encouraged me in the beginning of my attempts to learn how to pray. John Mogabgab, the editor of *Weavings*, has nurtured and encouraged me as a writer. Lillian Miao, the CEO of Paraclete Press, asked me to expand a *Weavings* article into a book, and Lil Copan, Acquisitions Editor, has helped me make it a better book. I thank Sr. Cor, Ellen, and Kent, my spiritual directors over the years, who have encouraged me to look carefully at God's call to abandonment and the ways I have of avoiding it. Thanks also go to Suanne, Paul, Bruce, Dorothy, Jen, and Warren from the clergy lectionary study group (and other colleagues from earlier groups) for constantly pushing me for clear statements of my understanding of theology and spirituality. Anna, Ruth, Anna Mary, Jeanne, and Anna, the members of the Prayer Group at Fifth Street United Methodist Church, have patiently listened to early drafts of the chapters. Carola, my wife, has read everything and made invaluable suggestions, both for the book and for my life. And Laura has put up with all the moving and distress that go with being a pastor's daughter and has come out of it all a wonderful young woman.

Preface

·

FOR THE LAST TWENTY YEARS OR SO, I've been praying a prayer called the Covenant Prayer. Its words are taken from a book by Richard Alleine, a Puritan minister of the mid-seventeenth century. The prayer itself is the creation of twentieth-century British Methodists and came to American Methodism in the 1960s. This book comes out of my reflections on praying the Covenant Prayer.

So why should you read it? Especially, why should you read it if you're not a Methodist? I can think of two good reasons.

First, the theme of the prayer is surrender to God, self-abandonment. Since that's one of the key themes of Christian spirituality, it's certainly worthwhile to spend some time thinking about it. You might find my successes and failures, my stumbling ways of avoiding total surrender, instructive. You might even recognize something of yourself in my excuses and my aspirations. At the very least, my reflections on this prayer that I pray may help you to pay more attention to the prayers that you pray, from table grace to the Lord's Prayer. And you may decide to make the Covenant Prayer a touchstone for your life, a constant reminder of your desire to commit yourself fully to following your own divine call to submit to God's will.

Second, the Covenant Prayer has become a sort of Grand Central Station where many trains of thought from spiritual classics come together for me. So during the course of this book you'll have a chance to meet or revisit some fascinating folks. The Carmelites are very well represented: Teresa of Avila, John of the Cross, Thérèse de Lisieux. They've really spoken to my heart. But you'll also meet Quaker John Woolman, Jesuits Jean-Pierre de Caussade and Thomas Green, and, of course, Richard Alleine. If a taste of them here makes you hungry for more, then this book could be the starting point for an exciting voyage of discovery.

Introduction

WE'VE HEARD THE CALL to surrender ourselves to God, from preachers and evangelists, in Sunday worship, at revivals, even watching television. Though the call comes in many forms, it always sounds so simple. Just turn your life over to Jesus. Say "Yes" to God. Let Jesus take control. Our responses can be just as varied. We might be led in the traditional prayer, "Jesus Christ, I accept you as my Lord and Savior." Or we might cry out as Keith Miller did, "God, if there's anything you want in this stinking soul, take it."[1] This is the basic decision of the spiritual life. Are we going to trust God or not? Will we seek to discern and to do God's will, or will we continue to insist that we know what's best for ourselves? The question is simple to ask, and the answer is a simple choice. But it is by no means easy to live it out.

"If God is for us," asks Paul, "who is against us?" He probably intended it as a rhetorical question. But his premise is yet another form of the fundamental question. Is God really for us? Or have we been abandoned by God, left alone and helpless in an uncaring universe, forced to fend for ourselves? We have to answer that question before we can go on to the choice to give

ourselves to God, to Christ, in self-abandonment. We
may answer with a confident, "Yes, God is for us. We
can trust God's loving guidance." Even then it can be
a journey of a lifetime to move from a decision that
God is trustworthy to actually trusting God.

The first step in this spiritual journey is from *ought*
to *want*. Before we know God at all, others tell us
about God and about what our relationship to God
should be. It can be a gentle suggestion or a demand:
"You really ought to trust God and trust yourself to
God." Eventually, whether by some experience of
God's love or from the realization that our attempts to
be good on our own are doomed to futility, we begin
to internalize the suggestion. We realize that we do
want to trust God to guide us in our lives. For some
people the realization comes gradually. For others it is
a single dramatic step, a conversion. But however we
come to want to trust God's guidance, we are soon
faced with another problem. While we may want to
trust God completely, we don't. At least I don't. I hold
back whole areas of my life from God's control. I try
hard to follow what I can see of God's plan for me in
some areas. In others I still second-guess every hint of
God's will. I may even openly reject what I'm sure God
wants of me. And so there needs to be a second step—
the slow, often painful movement from *want* to *be*.
Gradually we learn to trust God more and more, until
what we want has come to be who we are, until with

God we will one will. That is, until in cooperation with God's grace we have been made perfect in love.

Throughout this journey we need all the help we can get: encouragement from friends, spiritual guidance, support from a small group of fellow travelers, immersion in Scripture and other spiritual reading. But it is good to have some constant goad, something to push us forward toward the goal, to keep reminding us of the choice we've made. In *A Lesson Before Dying*, by Ernest J. Grimes, the members of a small African-American church all had their chosen 'Termination Songs, songs such as "Amazing Grace" or "Were You There," that they sang to express their determination to keep on loving and following Jesus until they see him in heaven, "where they were determined to spend eternity."[2] For the last quarter century or so, I have had a determination prayer to remind me to keep on keeping on. It is the Covenant Prayer.

I first met the Covenant Prayer in seminary. One of our chapel services was a service of covenant renewal. The climax of the service was a prayer I'd never seen before:

I am no longer my own, but thine.

Put me to what thou wilt,

rank me with whom thou wilt;

put me to doing, put me to suffering;

let me be employed for thee or laid aside for thee,

exalted for thee or brought low for thee;

let me be full, let me be empty;
let me have all things, let me have nothing;
I freely and heartily yield all things
to thy pleasure and disposal.
And now, O glorious and blessed God,
Father, Son, and Holy Spirit,
thou art mine, and I am thine.
So be it.
And the covenant which I have made on earth,
let it be ratified in heaven.
Amen.[3]

I learned later that the service was based on "An Order of Worship for Such as Would Enter into or Renew Their Covenant with God" from *The Book of Worship for Church and Home,* the official worship book of The United Methodist Church at that time. There it was commended for use as a Watch Night service for New Year's Eve. I filed the service away in the back of my mind as something I'd like to try some-day when I had my own parish.

A few years later, I was a pastor. I decided to try a service of covenant renewal, not as a Watch Night service, but as the regular morning service for the Sunday after New Year's Day. This time the Covenant Prayer made more of an impression. I was using a highly structured method—that's why we're called Methodists—for my personal morning and evening prayer. I decided to add the Covenant Prayer to that structure. I saw it as a way of carrying the essence of the renewal service with me through the year.

The next summer, I was ordained elder. Bishop Ault presented the three of us in my ordination group with beautifully calligraphed copies of the Covenant Prayer. I hung mine on the wall of my prayer closet. With this reinforcement, I continued to make the Covenant Prayer part of my daily devotions. I would like to be able to say that it has been a constant part of my prayer life ever since. Alas, nothing has really been constant. But self-abandonment to God has been a recurring theme—and a growing one—over the last twenty-some years. And so I keep coming back to the Covenant Prayer as a crystallization of that theme. I've recited it, reflected on it, studied it, even preached and lectured on it. The subjects of the study—the biblical background of covenant renewal, Alleine's call to full commitment in a solemn act of covenant, the development of a service of renewal in Methodism that led to the creation of the prayer—are treated in Appendix A. The reflections inspired the body of this book.

Even after years of living with the Covenant Prayer, sometimes it is just a prayer I repeat, almost without thinking. And sometimes it is the spur for deeper meditation. But always it reminds me of my deepest desire: to give up clinging to the illusion that I am my own and to become, by God's grace, fully God's.

By now you might be wondering, "Why bother with reciting a prayer at all? Shouldn't we move beyond such things to 'higher' forms of prayer like meditation and contemplation?" Well, yes, that's where we want to head. But the prayers we say, verbal or vocal prayers, are a doorway to these other forms of prayer. And they're a doorway we all pass through.

As children we begin with very simple prayers. I remember my grandfather at family gatherings for dinner, mumbling at length something about "heavenly juice." (Later I learned that his table grace began, "Bless this food to thy heavenly use. . . .") But I learned a simpler grace: "God is great, God is good, and we thank him for our food." It's a really good prayer. It covers the basics of praise and thanksgiving. And if you add the second stanza—"By his hands we all are fed. Give us, Lord, our daily bread"—you've included an affirmation of divine providence and a basic petition borrowed from the Lord's Prayer. For bedtime, I learned, "Now I lay me down to sleep. I pray the Lord my soul to keep. If I should die before I wake, I pray the Lord my soul to take." This was the first prayer of self-abandonment I learned. These simple children's prayers are really profound when we stop to analyze them.

The problem, of course, is that as children we spent little time in theological reflection. We just learned to say our prayers, by rote, in sing-songy haste. My parents may have tried to explain the meaning, but I don't remember such discussions. Even so, the words sank deep into my heart, and with them the key ideas of God's goodness and loving care, of how it was my duty and privilege to give thanks and commit myself into God's hands. And so they became forming centers for my spiritual development. Any later questioning was in light of these basic ideas. Garrison Keillor says that in Lake Woebegon, all the Norwegians were Lutherans, "even the atheists—it was a Lutheran God they did not believe in."[4] This is the effect of our earliest formation through the prayers we say and the songs we sing.

As we grow older, we learn to say other prayers. Foremost among these is the Lord's Prayer. Since it is a regular part of most Christian worship, we may hear it and mumble along before we have any idea what the words really are. Even as adults, the Lord's Prayer is often one giant word, beginning "Arfatherooardinevvin. . . ." When we attempt to slow down and think about what we're saying, we get lost. Or try to change the words from what we have learned, and we suddenly can't remember it at all.

I've had parishioners ask why we bothered to say the Lord's Prayer in worship. After all, they said, folks were just muttering their way through it without even noticing what they were saying. Why not drop it and say a different prayer each week, so we'd have to pay attention to the words? Rather than simply give up on such a central prayer, though, I looked for ways to recover it. One step was to slow down when I led the prayer in worship or in meetings. Another was to preach a series of sermons on its meaning. In addition, I made the Lord's Prayer the center of all our prayer, not only in worship, but as the closing of every meeting or Bible study. And this seemed to help. What we needed was not to pray different prayers, but to pay more attention to the prayer we already knew.

Such increased attention is how prayers move from rote repetition to formative power in our lives. When Teresa of Avila was asked how to move beyond vocal prayer to mental prayer, her advice was simple: think about what you're saying. "Mental prayer involves thinking about what we're saying, understanding it, realizing to Whom we are speaking, and asking ourselves how we dare to speak to so great a Lord."[5] As we accept the work of paying attention to what we are saying, particularly when praying in private, we move deeper and deeper into prayer. Teresa assures her sisters, ". . . while you are repeating the Paternoster or some other vocal prayer, the Lord might quite possibly grant you perfect contemplation."[6] That is, God may respond to our reflection on what we are saying by catching us up into a wordless, simple abiding in God's love.

Notice that Teresa does not limit such deepening of prayer to the Lord's Prayer. Certainly it is a standard prayer, known by all Christians. So there are a great many commentaries that help us to think about what we say, to give us food for thought. But, as I mentioned above, even a simple table grace can be a basis for profound reflection. There is similar depth in the Serenity Prayer, the Jesus Prayer, and the modern prayer based on the "Admonitions" of Francis of Assisi that begins, "Lord, make me an instrument. . . ." Any of these brief prayers can become a doorway into deeper prayer, a center of formation in our lives.

One of the first things that happens when we begin to slow down and pay attention to what we are saying in verbal prayer is that the prayer begins to speak to us, as well as to God. The prayer becomes a channel for two-way communication. We pray, "Thy kingdom come, thy will be done," and then we notice the ways in which God's will is not being done in our own lives and hear a call to be (to act as) extensions of God's reign—ambassadors for Christ. We pray, "Forgive us . . . as we forgive," and we see scenes of our own unforgiving behavior played out in our memories. We become aware of hurts long past that still fester in us. We try the Orthodox practice of repeatedly praying, "Lord Jesus Christ, Son of God, have mercy on me, a sinner." Suddenly we realize that we really are sinners and that all we have going for us is the mercy of our Lord Jesus. In the morning, we pray, "Lord, make me an instrument of your peace." Through the rest of the day, with each temptation to get caught up in an argument, a fight, a vehement debate, we remember what we have asked for—and maybe stop to ask again. The prayers we speak to God become God's response to us.

The bulk of this book is my own reflection on praying the Covenant Prayer and trying to live out God's call through it. Some of what follows is how God has spoken through the prayer in various situations. Other parts show how the prayer has become a nexus, a point of intersection and connection, for many things I have learned about the Christian spiritual life. This is how the Covenant Prayer has come to be my special doorway into deeper prayer, my own forming center.

By now I've already mentioned spiritual formation several times, as well as talking about a prayer becoming a formative center or having formative power. If such talk leaves you a little confused and wondering what spiritual formation is, you might want to jump ahead to Appendix B and read it now. If you have a pretty clear picture of spiritual formation, I'll just offer a brief reminder of one point.

Our spiritual growth tends to happen in fits and starts, as some event makes us painfully aware that our surface self is not fully in tune with God's call to us and may be no more than a patched together mass of contradictions. Faced with a new circumstance, this surface self won't hold together, and we must make some change (major or more likely very minor) in our way of life. This new "self" or current form will keep us going until the next crisis moves us to further adjustment.

The prayers that we pray can become a rock to which we cling through the storms of crisis. If they are basic prayers from our Christian tradition, we can be confident that they express, at least in part, God's call to us. Since they are prayers we have chosen and reaffirmed, we know that they express our own deepest longings and the core of our faith. As such, they are not simply aspects of our current form, but more fundamental expressions of the enduring core of who we are, our spiritual heart. That is why we speak of such prayers as being formative centers. They are the continuing vision of consonance around which we can build our new current life form. They are one of the truest expressions of who we hope to be. And so our reflections on them become a guide to how we need to grow.

Surrender

I AM NO LONGER MY OWN,
BUT THINE.

Put me to what thou wilt,

rank me with whom thou wilt;

put me to doing, put me to suffering;

let me be employed for thee or laid aside for thee,

exalted for thee or

brought low for thee;

let me be full, let me be empty;

let me have all things, let me have nothing;

I freely and heartily yield all things to thy

pleasure and disposal.

And now, O glorious and blessed God,

Father, Son, and Holy Spirit,

thou art mine, and I am thine.

So be it.

And the covenant which I have made

on earth, let it be ratified in heaven.

Amen.

CHAPTER 1

Surrender

I am no longer my own, but thine.

THE BEGINNING OF SURRENDER, or self-abandonment, is in knowing whose we are, whose I am. The trend today is to talk about our own choice to offer ourselves to God: "the day I made my decision for Christ." We sound as if we had carefully reviewed our choices and then had decided, calmly and rationally, to invest our time and our faith in Jesus and the God he spoke of. The problem with this approach is that we can easily view the God we have chosen as no longer God's own but ours, our personal property. We see God as a sort of giant vending machine into which we put our good deeds, in expectation of some blessing falling down for us to claim. And, of course, if the blessings are not vended, we kick the machine. God did not deliver as advertised, and we regret our choice.

In truth, though, the initiative is always God's. God laid claim to us long before we accepted that claim. We have always belonged to God anyway, whether we were willing to admit it or not. We are God's creatures. We exist, the universe exists, only because of God's ongoing creation. We were never really our own, but always have been God's. God states that claim clearly through the prophet: "But now thus says the LORD, he who created you, O Jacob, he who formed you, O Israel: Do not fear for I have redeemed you; I have called you by name, you are mine" (Isaiah 43:1). God then promises to be with God's people, to rescue them, to bring them home. Why? "Because you are precious in my sight, and honored, and I love you . . ." (Isaiah 43:4a). We are God's children, and God can no more forget us or give up on us than a mother would forget the child she bore (Isaiah 49:15).

We are Christ's by redemption. When in our attempts to be our own persons, we ended up selling ourselves to some other god (food, success, sex, power, computer games, security, whatever), Christ paid the price to buy us back. Paul asks the folks in Corinth, "Do you not know that your body is a temple of the Holy Spirit within you, which you have from God, and that you are not your own? For you were bought with a price; therefore glorify God in your body" (1 Corinthians 6:19–20). With Paul we must say, "It is no longer I who live, but it is Christ who lives in me. And the life I now live in the flesh I live by faith in the Son of God, who loved me and gave himself for me" (Galatians 2:20). We are no longer our own, but Christ's.

4

Even what good we have done is not strictly our own doing. For the Holy Spirit is working within us to guide, transform, encourage, teach. The best that we do is what we do when we cooperate with the Spirit. Even our assurance that we are God's beloved children is "that very Spirit bearing witness with our spirit that we are children of God" (Romans 8:16). We no longer claim our own accomplishments, but they are the Spirit's doing.

We have been made, claimed, redeemed, transformed by God—loving Parent, Jesus Christ, Holy Spirit. If we are to be honest at all, we each have to say, "I am no longer my own, but thine."

I can understand all of this intellectually and affirm it as truth. But still there is a part of me that rebels, that childishly shouts, "Oh yeah? Well, you're not the boss of me!" Or maybe it more poetically asserts, "I am the master of my fate; I am the captain of my soul!"[1] This is the part that hears God's call to unconditional love and asks, "What's in it for me?" It hears God's offer of absolute forgiveness and says, "If forgiveness is for everybody, then it's just not fair. After all, I'm pretty good and you're not so bad, but he's a real rat. Why should we all get the same deal?" Adrian van Kaam calls this deep-seated part of ourselves the pride form: "It veils the truth of our being made in God's image and likeness; . . . it tempts us with the illusion that we can do it alone; it encourages us to deny our dependency on the God who made us."[2] Thomas Merton calls it the false self. In the seventh chapter of Romans, Paul tries a number of names: sin, flesh, another law. He spells out clearly the warfare between the truth to which we give intellectual assent and the pride form:

> Now if I do what I do not want, it is no longer I that do it, but sin that dwells within me. So I find it to be a law that when I want to do what is good, evil lies close at hand. For I delight in the law of God in my inmost self, but I see in my members another law at war with the law of my mind, making me captive to the law of sin that dwells in my members. Wretched man that I am! Who will rescue me from this body of death? (Romans 7:20–24)

This is the conflict so often depicted in cartoons. A little angel-duck stands on Donald's left shoulder, a little demon-duck on his right shoulder, and they argue back and forth about what Donald should do. And even though it is presented as an inner struggle, the real decision is whether to follow God or rebel against God. The inner battle is truly a war of rebellion.

Such a rebellion can only end in unconditional surrender, self-surrender. "I tried to do it my way. It didn't work very well. I give up. I'll try to listen better this time, to follow your lead, Lord. I surrender." When I was starting in the ministry, I had a chance to talk with

Harry, whose ministry had begun in the early years of the twentieth century. He said that when he was a boy, self-surrender was a big theme in preaching, especially evangelistic preaching. People sang hymns like "I Surrender All," written in 1897, or "Trust and Obey," written ten years earlier. But then, said Harry, it all changed. America won the First World War. We were the top nation, the most powerful on earth. We didn't surrender to anyone. And so the language of surrender disappeared from mainstream American churches. At least that's what Harry said, and he was there. Maybe that's when we began to elevate our own choice, our "decision for Christ," as something made calmly and rationally, rather than as an admission of the truth to which our failures drove us.

The language of surrender is growing in popularity again. Maybe we realize how much we've mucked up trying to be in charge, or maybe the decline of the mainstream churches and the growth of evangelical ones has forced us to take a new look at the older language. At any rate, "I Surrender All" is back in the United Methodist hymnal. But it's still a struggle to reconcile the competing directives of Christian self-surrender and American self-reliance. We sing our surrender to Christ in church and then talk about the importance of looking out for number one the rest of the week. And while we may talk about our desire to serve God, many of us are mostly interested in serving as advisors.

More recently, Christian talk of self-surrender has been under attack from another direction. People struggling to gain some small measure of control over their lives are not eager to give it up again, even to God. Too often, Christ's call to self-denial has been used by oppressors to keep the oppressed in their place. Men (like me) have used it against women. Whites (me again) have used it against blacks and other persons of color. The rich (I guess I qualify here, too) have used it against the poor: "Just grin and bear it. Think of it as your cross. Join your pain to the suffering of Christ. When you get to heaven, you'll be blessed."

Christ came to set us free from such hogwash. Against all those who have tried to co-opt obedience to Christ as obedience to them, Jesus says, "No one can serve two masters; for a slave will either hate the one and love the other, or be devoted to the one and despise the other" (Matthew 6:24). Or, as Richard Alleine says, "Christ will accept of no consent but in full, to all that he requires; he will be all in all, or he will be nothing."[3] Others may be able to control our bodies or our work, but they cannot control our allegiance or our love. They are for Christ alone. All other loves, however strong, must take second place. We are no longer our own, but his. We may feel called to put up with oppression for Jesus' sake, as an opportunity to love our enemies, to do good to those who hurt us, and to witness to the gospel. But such action is for those who have found strength in Christ, who know his love and are able to endure all things through its power. As soon as an oppressor begins to claim that if we don't submit, Christ won't love us any more, that person—or that oppressive system—has lost any claim to speak in the name of Jesus. For Christ sets us free from the terror of death, from the fear of divine punishment for sin. He gives us back our lives, so that we may freely surrender them to him.

And still we don't. No matter how much control we have over our lives, we find it hard to give it up. We can always find reasons to insist that we alone know what is best for ourselves. We are happy to accept suggestions from God, of course. We respect Christ greatly. But we reserve to ourselves the right to make the final decision. We back away from full surrender. At least in some areas of our lives, we are sure we know what's really best.

But the Covenant Prayer keeps calling me away from this misplaced self-confidence. It helps me remember that I haven't really done very well trying to call the shots in my life. Great plans turned to dust and ashes. When I thought I was grabbing for all the gusto, it turned out to be pretty tasteless. Trying to be my own didn't work. Time to admit it, wave the flag of surrender, and let God be in control. Hannah Whitall Smith spelled out this surrender in a prayer over a century ago:

Here, Lord, I abandon myself to thee. I have tried in every way I could think of to manage myself, and to make myself what I know I ought to be, but have always failed. Now I give it up to thee. Do thou take entire possession of me. Work in me all the good pleasure of thy will. Mold and fashion me into such a vessel as seemeth good to thee. I leave myself in thy hands, and I believe thou wilt, according to thy promise, make me into a vessel unto thy own honor, "sanctified, and meet for the master's use, and prepared unto every good work."[4]

In the *Spiritual Exercises*, Ignatius of Loyola, the sixteenth-century founder of the Society of Jesus (Jesuits) counseled his readers to offer everything to Christ as part of freeing themselves to accept his love. As part of that counsel, he wrote a simple and powerful prayer of surrender:

Take, Lord, and receive all my liberty, my memory, my understanding, and all my will—all that I have and possess. You, Lord, have given all that to me. I now give it back to you, O Lord. All of it is yours. Dispose of it according to your will. Give me your love and your grace, for that is enough for me.[5]

Even though the Covenant Prayer is the one I learned first, this prayer also keeps echoing in my mind, thanks in part to a beautiful musical setting by a twentieth-century Jesuit, John Foley.[6]

10

Though Christ demands complete, unconditional surrender, we continue to fight our losing battle, giving up just a bit at a time. Though I promise complete, unconditional surrender when I pray the Covenant Prayer, I constantly find new ways in which I am resisting God's will, new areas of my life that insist on having their own way. Surrender is not once and for all, but every day a little more. As John the Baptizer said, in a different context, "He must increase, but I must decrease" (John 3:30). I have made this verse into a breath prayer: "More of you, Lord, less of me." It serves as a reminder of my desire to surrender more fully throughout the day. It is also the mantra that I use for centering at the beginning of more formal prayer times.

John of the Cross, a sixteenth-century Carmelite and close associate of Teresa of Avila in her reform of the order, speaks of Christians as panes of glass through which the light of Christ shines. The dirtier the glass is, the more we see the glass and not the light. But when the pane is clear, transparent, the light blazes through in all its glory.

> A soul makes room for God by wiping away all the smudges and smears of creatures, by uniting its will perfectly to God's; for to love is to labor to divest and deprive oneself for God of all that is not God. When this is done the soul will be illumined by and

transformed in God. And God will so communicate his supernatural being to the soul that it will appear to be God himself and will possess what God himself possesses.[7]

Strangely enough, this transparency is not a loss of self, but the fullest realization of our calling. What we are losing is the pride form, the false self. As the false self disappears, it stops obscuring God's call to us and lets our true self, who we most deeply are, shine through along with the light of God. Church Father Irenaeus said that the glory of God is the truly living human person, and true human life consists in beholding God.[8] And we are most fully alive when we are most fully surrendered to Christ, when people look at us and see him in action. So as we surrender ourselves more and more fully, we give more glory to God.

God's Call

the covenant prayer

I am no longer my own,
but thine.
**PUT ME TO WHAT THOU WILT,
RANK ME WITH WHOM THOU WILT;**
put me to doing, put me to suffering;
let me be employed for thee or laid aside for thee,
exalted for thee or
brought low for thee;
let me be full, let me be empty;
let me have all things, let me have nothing;
I freely and heartily yield all things to thy
pleasure and disposal.
And now, O glorious and blessed God,
Father, Son, and Holy Spirit,
thou art mine, and I am thine.
So be it.
And the covenant which I have made
on earth, let it be ratified in heaven.
Amen.

CHAPTER 2

God's Call

Put me to what thou wilt, rank me with whom thou wilt.

AFTER THE OPENING STATEMENT of our determination to be God's rather than our own, the body of the Covenant Prayer falls into two main portions. The first several clauses deal with what we do—or how we are sometimes called to do nothing—and the status we gain (or lose) for our actions. The next few clauses focus instead on what we have or lack, both in blessings and in material things.

We begin, then, with the tasks to which God may put us. I have always had trouble making long-range plans. My parents claim that my earliest career goal was to be a trash collector. They went scurrying all over town trying to find the garbage truck I wanted for Christmas. By the time I was in elementary school, I wanted to be a doctor. By junior high school, though, I was pretty well set on computer programming. I even taught BASIC programming to the math teachers of my school when I was in ninth grade! That goal lasted on into college, where I graduated with a degree in computer science.

But even before I graduated, I was pretty sure that God was calling me into pastoral ministry. There were no dramatic visions—just a gut feeling that, while playing with computers might be fun and profitable, it would never be as fulfilling as the service of God. I thought that I knew what such service would be like, based on growing up in a large downtown congregation. Nothing in my college or seminary experience prepared me for the culture shock of being appointed to three rural churches in New York's Southern Tier. My congregations ranged in size from six to fifty. Folks were mostly farm families, storekeepers, truckers, construction workers. As near as I could tell, I'd been chosen for this place mostly because I played guitar and wore an alb, as had my beloved predecessor.

When my ministry failed to bring the countryside flocking into the churches, an older pastor consoled me with words of wisdom that his father had offered him when he started in ministry: "Well, if anything were going to happen in that place, you don't think they'd have put *you* there, do you?" That place wasn't the end of the world—even though it might have been the middle of nowhere. I should look on this appointment as a shakedown cruise, a chance to add practical experience to the theory of ministry I'd learned in seminary. In the meantime, I consoled myself (and some of the people consoled themselves) with the thought that in a few years I'd move on to someplace larger and more suited to my gifts and graces. And so I would continue onward and upward in my career as a pastor.

It was in this first parish that I began to pray the Covenant Prayer. "Put me to what thou wilt, rank me with whom thou wilt." This is the first of several lines in the prayer that spell out what belonging to God means, in terms of letting God guide our lives and our actions. If we are truly servants of Christ, we must do more than pick whatever work pleases us and offer it for his glory. We need to listen for God's instructions, to seek to learn what work God has chosen for us. Alleine spells out what obedience means for servants of Christ:

> They must not pick and choose: "This I will do and that I will not do." They must not say, "This is too hard," or "This is too mean," or "This may be well enough let alone." Good servants, when they have chosen their master, will let their master choose their work and will not dispute it.[1]

In the course of seeking to do the work to which God has put us, we are bound to make mistakes. God's direct call to us is buried so deeply in our hearts that we can hear it only partially, and then only through the distortions of many other directives we have taken into

our hearts from a variety of sources. Our own prefer-
ences may drown out God's call. We will do what we
want and hope that God wants it, too. We will try to
do what God wants, but in a way that suits us. We will
cling to our own plans and dreams as long as possible.
One time I was talking to an older pastor about some
of the dreams I had, of being a great writer or a great
singer. He asked, "What about being a great pastor?"
Without thinking, I snapped, "No, that's what God
wants me to do." It wasn't one of my finest moments.
As I realized what I had said, I knew that I still had a
long way to go in learning to let Christ be in control.

Alleine was very much aware of this mixture of
motives, of the depth of our desire to suit ourselves and
seek our own glory. He warned:

> Christ hath many services to be done. Some are
> more easy and honorable, others more difficult and
> disgraceful. Some are suitable to our inclinations
> and interests, others are contrary to both. In some
> we may please Christ and please ourselves. . . . But
> then there are other works wherein we cannot
> please Christ but by denying ourselves.[2]

The necessity to let Christ take charge is actually a
relief. He knows us better than we know ourselves.
The work that looks attractive to us may, in fact, be all
wrong for us. Or even though it may work out, it may
not be the best use of our spiritual gifts. If we let Christ

take charge, if we listen carefully for his direction, he will surely lead us into the work where we are needed and that we need for our own growth.

Now, twenty-three years after beginning in those three country churches, I am the pastor of a single church with an average attendance of forty-two. So much for glorious career plans! In the meantime, I've served several other parishes (some only part time), spent time back in school, done a fair amount of writing and editing. I've even been back to computers while my wife attended seminary. At one point I was convinced that I was finished being a pastor. Somewhere along the way, I gave up on the idea of trying to make career plans and admitted I was pretty much in the dark about my future.

The image of stumbling in the dark took shape in a meditation while I was in my second parish. My spiritual director had suggested a simple start for visualization. "Imagine yourself going down a long stairway into the ground and when you reach the bottom you find a door. Open it and see what you find." I followed the instructions and found myself in a large, dark cave. Stairs and door had vanished as soon as I entered. I had a small candle, but it scarcely lit the hand and arm holding it. I couldn't see the floor at all. From a computer adventure I'd been playing, I knew that if you walked in a dark cave without light, you'd fall into a pit and die, or else be eaten by a grue (the archetypal gruesome beasts that live in dark caves waiting for unwary travelers). I was afraid to move. But I knew enough about guided imagery meditation to ask for the help I needed. I asked for more light, so I could see where I was going. But that's not what I got. Instead a hand reached into my tiny ball of light, an offer of guidance. I became angry. I didn't want a guide through the dark. I wanted light—and maybe a map, too! I wanted to see where I was going, look over options, and make my own plans. And with that the meditation ended.

The Covenant Prayer calls me to accept the guiding hand. "Put me to what thou wilt, rank me with whom thou wilt." Abandonment means not only that there is no promise of a map, there's no hope of one. Jean-Pierre de Caussade, in his classic *Abandonment to Divine Providence*, seems to speak directly to my meditation.

> Imagine we are in a strange district at night and are crossing fields unmarked by any path, but we have a guide. He asks no advice nor tells us of his plans. So what can we do except trust him? It is no use trying to see where we are, look at maps, or question passers-by. That would not be tolerated by a guide who wants us to rely on him. He will get satisfaction from overcoming our fears and doubts, and will insist that we have complete trust in him.[3]

Of course, God's guidance is rarely as clear and direct as a guiding hand. At times it has seemed much more like a quiet voice whispering, "Over this way . . . that's right . . . you're getting warmer . . . no, now you've wandered off course." Sometimes I've mistaken echoes for the source of the voice and found myself completely lost. Following such guidance requires constant attentiveness and a readiness at any moment to change direction radically. In another extended metaphor, Caussade compares this to trying to steer a small boat in changing winds:

> When the wind is shifting, one can be sure of its direction only from moment to moment. So it is with these souls. They too have their course continually altered by the will of God, and his will can be understood only by its effects, by what it accomplishes in these souls either through secret, hidden promptings or through the duties of their state of life.[4]

Hidden promptings and duties—God's guidance in many tiny incidents—have made for radical changes of direction in my life. A gut feeling led me to seminary. An invitation to guest preach in a small church led to a year as interim pastor of that congregation. A suggestion that I look on a small parish as an opportunity to do some studying led to six years of commuting to Duquesne University's Institute of Formative Spirituality and new ways of looking at spiritual formation. An invitation to review books by Ron DelBene reshaped my prayer life. A lunchtime conversation about an old series of selections from spiritual classics turned into becoming the editor of a new series, the fifteen volumes (so far) of *The Upper Room Spiritual Classics*. And so, while I have no clue what lies ahead, I've learned to enjoy stumbling along in the dark, trying to follow my guide. Sometimes it even feels a little like dancing.

Still, that meditation haunted me. I even tried to redo it, to give up my anger and take the offered hand; but it always seemed forced. And then one day when I was describing the meditation, my wise friend Janet asked, "Why do you think those are the only two options?" After sitting in stunned silence for a little while, I accepted her challenge to be creative. So, when I had time, I tried the meditation one more time. But this time, when the hand reached into the little globe of light, I grabbed it, dropped the candle, and pulled my guide into an embrace. And together we sat down in the darkness. What I really needed was just to spend some time getting to know the guide or even just to be with him. And then I was ready to follow his lead.

Acceptance

the covenant prayer

I am no longer my own,
but thine.
Put me to what thou wilt,
rank me with whom thou wilt;
**PUT ME TO DOING,
PUT ME TO SUFFERING;**
let me be employed for thee or laid aside for thee,
exalted for thee or
brought low for thee;
let me be full, let me be empty;
let me have all things, let me have nothing;
I freely and heartily yield all things to thy
pleasure and disposal.
And now, O glorious and blessed God,
Father, Son, and Holy Spirit,
thou art mine, and I am thine.
So be it.
And the covenant which I have made
on earth, let it be ratified in heaven.
Amen.

CHAPTER 3

Acceptance

Put me to doing, put me to suffering.

THIS PHRASE AND THE NEXT SPELL out what it means to say, "Put me to what thou wilt." First is a declaration of our willingness to be put to doing or to suffering, as God sees fit. The suffering here is not *being-in-pain*. Rather, it is *being-done-to*, allowing things to happen, or enduring while things happen that are completely beyond our control. Think of the confusing command in Mark 10:14 in the King James Version: "Suffer the little children to come unto me, and forbid them not." It doesn't mean "try to endure having kids around," but simply, "allow them to come." In Matthew's version of the baptism of Jesus, John the Baptist protests. Matthew 3:15 (KJV) reads, "And Jesus answering said unto him, 'Suffer it to be so now: for thus it becometh us to fulfill all righteousness.' Then he suffered him." Which, being interpreted, means, "And Jesus answered, 'That's the way it's got to be. Deal with it.' And John caved."

The suffering to which God may put us can take many different forms. Suffering can certainly include enduring through a painful illness or recovery from an injury. But it could also mean waiting for a baby to be born, or for a light to change, or for a doctor to emerge from an operating room with a report. Suffering can be waiting to hear whether you are included in the latest round of layoffs at your company, or if your application has been accepted and you have a new job. It can also be simple permission, bowing to another's will rather than insisting on your own, as when John let Jesus have his way and baptized him. Life is full of this kind of suffering.

The prayer, then, calls us to accept this suffering, this *being-done-to*, as God's gift to us, just as much as calls to action. We might even paraphrase, "Put me to activity, put me to passivity." In the last chapter I talked about being put to activity. This, of course, involves its own sort of passivity, waiting for God's guidance, standing still in the darkness until the hand reaches for us. But even then we long for that direction, we long to be put to some sort of activity. It is easy for us to pray, "Put me to doing."

Accepting passivity is much more difficult, let alone praying to be put to it. We learn from an early age that passivity—idleness or lack of control—is a bad thing. Idle hands, we are told, are the devil's playground. Employees at McDonald's (the first employer of more Americans than any other company) were taught, "If there's time enough to lean, there's time enough to clean." We try to fill up the dead times in our lives. We read or chat while waiting in line, flip through ancient magazines in doctors' waiting rooms, fume and pound the steering wheel at stop lights. Men used to be told to boil water during a birth as much to give them something to do and to get them out of the way as for any need for quantities of boiling water. Rather than stare at my computer screen while I wait for inspiration for the next sentence I must write, I switch windows and play another game of FreeCell—anything rather than sit idle.

And yet passivity is a major part of every life. Sometimes there is nothing we can do. Sometimes God puts us to waiting, to enduring, to being done to. And then abandonment to God means waiting, enduring, letting things happen. Thomas Merton tells a story from his early days at Gethsemani. The monastery had purchased exhaust fans that required creating holes in the roof.

> . . . Two frail novices who are very young were post-ed down on the ground floor near the doorways with artistic signs which read "Falling Bricks." At first one of them was standing at the precise spot where all the falling bricks would land on his head. He was saying the rosary in an attitude of perfect abandonment.[1]

Sometimes prayer and abandonment are the only appropriate responses to God's call to suffering. The prime example for Christians is Christ's own prayer in the Garden of Gethsemane: "Abba, Father, for you all things are possible; remove this cup from me; yet not what I want, but what you want" (Mark 14:36). Up to this point in the Gospel, Jesus has been very active, traveling all over Galilee to teach and heal, coming to Jerusalem, teaching in the temple. But from this point on, Jesus is acted upon rather than acting. He even stops his disciples from trying to take action. His passivity increases through the rest of the passion story (passion and passivity come from the same root word). Although "He never said a mumblin' word" is not quite accurate, Jesus speaks rarely and never in order to grab back control. He is hauled from place to place, beaten, and finally nailed to a cross, unable to move, completely exposed. All he can do is make one final prayer of surrender: "Father, into your hands I commend my spirit" (Luke 23:46). And the passivity continues until he is raised from the dead. Note even here the use of the passive voice: "is raised" not "rose"—at least in the overwhelming majority of references to the Resurrection in the New Testament. Jesus was put to suffering—God put Jesus to suffering—that only ended when he "was raised from the dead by the glory of the Father," as Paul puts it in Romans 6:4. And then, once more, God put him to doing.

Most of us (thank God) are never called to such great suffering. Our waiting, enduring, surrendering control, are on a much smaller scale. Even if we have to endure great pain, it is usually with the support of friends and the assistance of doctors and nurses, not alone, exposed, reviled. But still there come times, maybe even long stretches, when all we can do is say, "Let it be done to me according to your will, God." Or perhaps our prayer is more, "Let whatever happens to me be somehow in harmony with your will—or at least something you can use for good."

One such time in my life, one that recurs every few years, is waiting for news of a new pastoral appointment. That's the way it works for United Methodist clergy: the bishop appoints us to a parish. We are allowed some input as to what sort of place we would like to be in, but the bishop is free to give our preference great weight or little in making the assignment. Since I have never come close to guessing where I would be sent, there is little point to fretting about it. I might as well just pray the Covenant Prayer and pray for the Spirit to guide the decision. The appointive system can be excellent training in abandonment and in suffering. During a couple of these times of waiting, my breath prayer was, "Jesus, teach me how to love." In the context of abandonment, this meant accepting everything that came my way as a learning opportunity, one more way for Jesus to teach me. Of course, having put the appointive process in this context, I had little room to second-guess the result. I can only accept that whatever happens is what God would have me do, at least for the next little while. Once I give up thoughts of career advancement and concentrate only on growth in abandonment, even the worst situations can be received as God's gift. All my appointments have had something to teach me both about being a pastor and about living in abandonment to divine providence. Sometimes I have needed a good bit of distance to gain the perspective to see what I've been taught.

Talking about a season of suffering is talking about a quality to life that endures over an extended period of time. While I waited to hear about an appointment, I was still actively working as a student, a pastor, a customer service rep, a writer. I had plenty to do. But behind all the doing was an intense feeling of waiting. Mourning can also be a season of suffering. When my mother died, the world didn't stop so I could mourn. I was still a pastor, a student, a husband, and a father. But I was a pastor *whose mother had just died*, a student *whose mother had died*, etc. I continued to preach and teach in my parish, to study and write papers for my classes. But I was never far from a sense of grief, coupled with anger at God. For weeks that stretched into months I was busy going on with my life, but afraid to pray, afraid to unleash my anger. Finally a friend urged me to go ahead and be mad. God could take it. This was yet another part of my life I had to surrender to God, another step in abandonment. And so even this season of suffering passed.

One form of being-done-to that comes to all of us, if we live long enough, is aging. We can fight it with exercise, cosmetics, even surgery. We can use hair color (if there's any left to color) or rugs, transplants, and drugs to fight or disguise baldness. We can "think young," try to keep up with the latest music, seek younger sexual partners, and generally make fools of ourselves. We deny, deny, deny. We try hard to follow Dylan Thomas's advice:

> Do not go gentle into that good night,
> Old age should burn and rave at close of day;
> Rage, rage against the dying of the light.[2]

But no matter how we rage, deny, disguise, exercise, and eat healthy, we still grow older. It will happen to us no matter what we do. I see myself turning into my father: same bald head, same pear-shaped profile— brought home much too clearly in a recent photo of the two of us facing each other. I can look at him and get a thirty-year forecast, including probabilities of heart trouble and glaucoma. Or I can look at the people of my church and see a broad spectrum of aging, including folks in their eighties who seem much younger than others in their sixties. But even though the experience is different for each one, we'll all get older and slowly lose the ability to do things we once took for granted: reading books, going for walks, remembering names, keeping track of time.

And so we can rage or we can once again surrender our aging to God. This is not the same as giving up and acting feeble before we need to. Rather it is accepting that aging is part of life and that God is still working with us and in us, despite what is happening to our bodies and minds. John Yungblut (borrowing a phrase from Teilhard de Chardin) speaks of hallowing our diminishments. This begins with deep, creative acceptance of our diminishments as companions who will be with us through the rest of our journey "to accompany [us] on [our] way to the great diminishment, death."[3] He continues, "Treating one's diminishments as companions affords one a certain detachment from them which in turn allows one to exercise a kind of playfulness in relationship to them, to maintain a sense of humor about them."[4] Later, Yungblut quotes a prayer by Teilhard de Chardin, taken from *The Divine Milieu*:

> When the signs of age begin to mark my body (and still more when they touch my mind), when the ill that is to diminish me or carry me off strikes from without or is born within me; when the painful moment comes in which I suddenly awaken to the fact that I am ill or growing old; and above all at that last moment when I feel I am losing hold of myself and am absolutely passive within the hands of the great unknown forces that have formed me,

in all these dark moments, O God, grant that I may understand that it is you (provided only my faith is strong enough) who is painfully parting the fibers of my being in order to penetrate to the very marrow of my substance and bear me away within yourself.[5]

Prayer itself can be a training ground for waiting, for passivity. Of course, there is active prayer, prayer that is giving God our to-do list or prayer that is pouring out our hearts before God. But there is also prayer that is passive, that does nothing except *be* in God's presence. A few years ago, I discovered a new psalm. Maybe I'd just never noticed it before, but it certainly seemed that someone had snuck it into the psalter when I wasn't looking. It is Psalm 131 (using the marginal reading in verse 2):

> O LORD, my heart is not lifted up,
>> my eyes are not raised too high;
> I do not occupy myself with things
>> too great and too marvelous for me.
> But I have calmed and quieted my soul,
>> like a weaned child with its mother;
>> my soul within me is like a weaned child.
> O Israel, hope in the LORD
>> from this time on and forevermore.

What a wonderful image of prayer! Not trying to run the world or give God advice. Not thinking deep theological thought in meditation. Just sitting in

Mommy's lap like a little child. Like a *weaned* child, that is, a child who doesn't need to be in Mommy's lap to nurse, but is just there because it's a good, comfortable, and comforting place to be. Prayer can be not doing anything but simply resting in God's arms, God's lap—maybe even falling asleep.

This is the kind of prayer that Thomas Green has in mind when he calls prayer "wasting time with God" or "floating." He talks first about his experiences trying to teach people to float in water.

> [I]t is puzzling to see what a difficult art floating really is—difficult not because it demands much skill but because it demands much letting go. The secret of floating is in learning *not* to do all the things we instinctively want to do. We want to keep ourselves rigid, ready to save ourselves the moment a big wave comes along—and yet the more rigid we are the more likely we are to be swamped by the waves; if we relax in the water we can be carried up and down by the rolling sea and never be swamped.[6]

Later he adds, "To learn to float, it seems, is essentially to learn to trust, first the teacher and then the water."[7] It is a matter of learning to be at home in the water.

So it is with prayer. Too many of us learn prayer only as something to get through in order to accomplish something with God. But it can be a time of floating, of profound resting, of being "at home in the sea that is God, with no visible means of support except the water whose ebb and flow, whose sudden surgings, we cannot predict or control."[8] The spoken prayer "put me to suffering" can become an invitation to wait upon the Lord or, better still, to wait with the Lord, just enjoying the time together.

Laid Aside

I am no longer my own,
but thine.
Put me to what thou wilt,
rank me with whom thou wilt;
put me to doing, put me to suffering;

**LET ME BE EMPLOYED FOR THEE
OR LAID ASIDE FOR THEE,**

exalted for thee or
brought low for thee;
let me be full, let me be empty;
let me have all things, let me have nothing;
I freely and heartily yield all things to thy
pleasure and disposal.
And now, O glorious and blessed God,
Father, Son, and Holy Spirit,
thou art mine, and I am thine.
So be it.
And the covenant which I have made
on earth, let it be ratified in heaven.
Amen.

CHAPTER 4

Laid Aside

Let me be employed for thee or laid aside for thee.

ALLOWING GOD TO PUT us to whatever God wills sometimes can mean being put to nothing at all, being laid
aside. A friend recently said to me, "When you're lying
in a hospital bed for chemotherapy because the cancer
has already metastasized, the idea of praying, 'Let me
be . . . laid aside for thee,' takes on a whole new
meaning." There are many ways we can find ourselves
laid aside. We can become suddenly ill. We can be laid
off or fired. Or we can come gradually to retirement
from our jobs or our other commitments and responsibilities. All of these possibilities give new meaning to
the idea of being laid aside. And all challenge us to
discover what it means to be laid aside for God's sake,
how this, too, can fit into God's plan for us.

I haven't had the personal experience of a long
illness—yet. But I have had enough friends go through
heart attacks and surgery, cancer treatments, recovery
from accidents, and the like, to know that the suffering
(both the pain and the surrendering of control) are not

the whole story. Several friends have expressed surprise at how easily the world went on without them. Pastors found that when they weren't around to do everything, lay people took up the slack, made visits, ran meetings, helped to lead worship with guest speakers. The humbling knowledge that we are not indispensable can be more of a blow than learning that we cannot take health for granted. This ego shock can be an opportunity to release the heavy, self-imposed burden of carrying the world on our shoulders. Being employed for God need not mean that we are personally responsible for everything God wants done in the world.

Carlo Carretto made this discovery after he had chosen a life of being laid aside. He had been a very active layperson, serving as the National President of Catholic Youth in Italy during his late thirties and early forties. Then in 1954, at the age of 44, he heard God calling him to leave everything and go into the desert of North Africa as one of the Little Brothers of Jesus. He describes a meditation in which he saw the whole of the Church "as a temple sustained by many columns, large and small, each one with the shoulder of a Christian under it."[1] This was an image he had carried for many years. But now, in a desert cave, he was ready to let go of the burden.

> I drew back suddenly, as though to free myself from this weight. What had happened? Everything

40

remained in its place, motionless. Not a movement,
not a sound. After twenty-five years I had realized
that nothing was burdening my shoulders and that
the column was my own creation—sham, unreal,
the product of my imagination and my vanity. . . .
The weight of the world was all on Christ Crucified.
I was nothing, absolutely nothing.[2]

After this revelation, Carretto was able to radically
re-order his life. He could burn his address book, give
up his need to be on top of things and in contact with
the world. He could be employed for God in a very different way, as one of the poorest of the poor, making
sandals out of old tires. And in that situation, he was
also a Christian among Muslims, living a simple witness
for Christ.

Sometimes being laid aside (whether voluntarily or
through sudden illness) can be a chance to let go of our
need to be in charge. We can step out from under the
pillars we have imagined, whether it is the Church or a
church or a business or a family we have been trying to
carry. No longer do we have to try to convince Christ
to accept the employment we have chosen, the burden
we have imposed on ourselves. We are set free to listen
to God and to discover the employment to which God
is calling us.

Of course, there are times when there seems to be
no new employment in the future, at least not in this

life. Senior citizens have consistently been the largest group in the churches I've served. Most of them have coped fairly well with the need to lay down the burden of their jobs in the world. They've reached retirement age, and many are glad to be able to relax and travel and draw the pension they've earned. Voluntary jobs, though, can be another matter entirely. Folks can see church jobs or offices as their chance to be employed for God, not just for themselves. In a society in which people are often defined by what they do, not to do anything can seem to mean being nobody, nothing. And so people cling to these last important tasks as long as possible, until failing eyesight makes it impossible to see the figures in a checkbook or failing memory makes mistakes too common.

The church I serve now is famous (at least in Harrisburg) for making chocolate eggs for Easter—peanut butter, butter cream, coconut, cherry, and mint. The project starts soon after New Year's Day and ends just before Holy Week. Working just two days a week, folks produce between 30,000 and 40,000 eggs. Very few of the workers are under seventy years old. Many are over eighty. The project began as a way of raising money for church youth bus trips, back when their own children were in the youth group. Each year they debate whether it's time to call it quits. But by fall, they are ready to try one more time. The church needs the money. And they need the activity and the fellowship.

They have found a way of being employed for God—even if only part time—and of continuing tasks from when they were younger. If they didn't make eggs, they might feel that they had been laid aside for God once and for all. And they're not ready for that yet.

Even when fingers cannot work and eyes cannot see, we can still be employed for Christ. We can pray. I have known folks who listened to police and fire scanners, not just to keep up with what was going on in the world, but to pray for those in trouble and those trying to help them. Others have used breath prayer as a form short enough to remember even when memory is failing.[3] Hymns can also be a form of prayer for the elderly. Sometimes folks who have lost the ability to speak through a stroke can still sing the hymns they learned as children, since singing and speaking use different parts of the brain. When John Wesley was dying, he began to sing a hymn by Isaac Watts:

> I'll praise my Maker while I've breath,
> And when my voice is lost in death,
> Praise shall employ my nobler powers;
> My days of praise shall ne'er be past,
> While life, and thought, and being last,
> Or immortality endures.[4]

At first, Wesley made it all the way through the verse. But as he grew weaker, he could only whisper, "I'll praise. . . . " He did, indeed, praise God while he had breath, employed for God to the end of his life, and confident of new and greater employment in the life to come.

Job loss can be a devastating form of being laid aside. My first job after college was for a small high-tech firm. Within two years, our main product line had been sold to a larger company and what was left of the company folded. So my first real employment became my first experience of being laid off. At least there it was quick, and I found a new job fairly quickly. In the church, being laid aside is a more drawn-out process. Like politicians, we can have a long period of being lame ducks.

In our United Methodist system, churches (and pastors) are asked in December whether they want a pastoral change, to begin the next July. That leaves half a year between request and change, which can be a time of goodbyes and celebrations of ministry. But I have also experienced this interim as a depressing time of trying to minister to folks who have rejected me. I have had three pastoral appointments that lasted one year. One was an intentional interim appointment, so I began to waddle and quack when I arrived. In another, it was soon obvious that the two churches could not afford a full-time pastor. In the third, there was simply a mismatch combined with miscommunication. I wasn't even sure I'd be able to stay for the whole year. I became so depressed that sometimes it was a major chore just to get out of bed in the morning. Of course, there were still some families that supported me, and they helped me to keep going. But it was rough. Since my wife was about to enter seminary, I couldn't face the idea of trying to start in a new parish on my own. So I took a leave of absence and went back to computers while Carola got her degree.

A few years ago I took another break from pastoral ministry to concentrate on writing. One year I was appointed as a quarter-time pastor (the interim appointment mentioned above), but mostly I was working on various projects for Upper Room Books. Even though I had work to do, my income—and therefore our family income—was down significantly. Every decision became a financial decision—could we afford what we wanted to do or buy. Even though I felt that the writing and editing I was doing was as surely being employed for God as my pastorates had been, I still felt angry about how little we could afford and guilty that my attempt to be a writer was causing the trouble. I took a temp job one year (data entry clerk) to help pay my daughter's college tuition. I sold my plasma twice a week to pay for movies and an occasional night out. And when one project was put "on hiatus" and others ended with nothing new on the horizon, I had to admit that maybe the impetus to move to this new form of ministry hadn't been God's call. I requested appointment as a pastor again.

Being laid aside can be a spiritual problem when it makes us re-evaluate our entire relationship to God. In the crisis of apparent career failure, all kinds of questions ran through my mind. If I had truly been employed for God, how could being laid aside, being rejected, be for God, too? If I was following God's call, why didn't things work out better? Or was I following my own will and deluding myself that my choices had anything to do with God's will? Had I ever heard God at all? Or was my whole life, my whole ministry self-deception? Did God really care at all? Or could it be that I had heard God's call clearly, but botched things up so badly that God was dumping me, giving up on me?

Or was there another possibility? Maybe being laid aside was just something that happened in a world by no means dedicated to following God's will, let alone to seeing God's will for me fulfilled. But as long as I was laid aside, I could offer the time to God, accept it as a chance to regroup, refocus, recommit. The Chinese character for "crisis" is made up of two simpler characters. One means "danger." The other means "opportunity." When we are employed, it is easy to assume that what we are doing is according to God's will for us and to keep going full speed ahead. But in the crisis of being laid aside, we can take the opportunity to ask the hard questions, to listen more closely for God's call. We have the chance to make small course corrections or major changes of direction, or simply to sit becalmed for a while until once again the Spirit blows us onward.

Once again I am a full-time pastor. Three years ago I would have told you that would never happen again. I am the pastor of a small community in a very large building. I can look back and see how my experiences have helped to prepare me for this parish. I have learned how to work with senior citizens, how to love small churches, how to offer hope rather than guilt in a time of decline. I am also writing a book and editing another. Maybe the problem wasn't misunderstanding my call at all. Maybe I just was foolish to think that anything was permanent, that I could foresee what was coming. Abandonment means listening each moment for God's new call, whether to new employment or to a time of being laid aside.

Status

I am no longer my own,
but thine.
Put me to what thou wilt,
rank me with whom thou wilt,
put me to doing, put me to suffering;
let me be employed for thee or laid aside for thee,

**EXALTED FOR THEE OR
BROUGHT LOW FOR THEE;**

let me be full, let me be empty;
let me have all things, let me have nothing;
I freely and heartily yield all things to thy
pleasure and disposal.
And now, O glorious and blessed God,
Father, Son, and Holy Spirit,
thou art mine, and I am thine.
So be it.
And the covenant which I have made
on earth, let it be ratified in heaven.
Amen.

CHAPTER 5

Status

Exalted for thee or brought low for thee . . .

Even if we are prepared for God to put us to doing or being-done-to or even not-doing, it can still be a challenge to accept whatever status, high or low, may come our way. We live in a success-oriented culture. We are told from early childhood to dream big. Even the Army tells us, "Be all that you can be." We frantically accumulate things, not because we need them, but because they are status symbols, signs of how exalted we have become. Without them, we believe we are nothing. Many years ago, I attended a retreat where Harry Raines was one of the speakers. He talked about his experiences working with laid-off steelworkers in Allentown, Pennsylvania. Throughout his talk ran a refrain, the dark underside of the American Dream: "This is America, where anybody can be Somebody. And if you're not Somebody, then you're nobody and you have nobody to blame but yourself." We long to be successful, to get rich, or at least to get our fifteen minutes of fame, even if it's only describing for the reporter from the Weather Channel what it was like when the tornado picked up our home and destroyed it. As the saying goes, it's better to be a Has-Been than a Never-Was.

Richard Alleine lived in a highly structured society, one very conscious of class. That is why he speaks of rank rather than status. "Rank me with whom thou wilt." That line is expanded in this one, the expression of willingness to be exalted or brought low for Christ. Actually, Alleine wrote "trodden underfoot." In a class-conscious society, rank is fixed by birth for most people. The key to life is not getting ahead, but rather knowing one's place and acting accordingly. If one is a servant, then being a good servant means doing the master's will in such a way that the master is exalted. And as long as the master is exalted, it truly doesn't matter whether the servant is the exalted head butler or is trodden underfoot as a stable hand or a scullery maid. Status, to the extent it matters at all, is the reflected status of the master.

This image of servant and master was already old when Jesus taught and healed in Galilee. Many of his parables and other sayings draw on the relationship between master and servant.

> Do you thank the slave for doing what was commanded? So you also, when you have done all that you were ordered to do, say, 'We are worthless

slaves; we have done only what we ought to have done!' (Luke 17:9–10)

You know that among the Gentiles, those whom they recognize as their rulers lord it over them, and their great ones are tyrants over them. But it is not so among you; but whoever wishes to become great among you must be your servant, and whoever wishes to be first among you must be slave of all. For the Son of Man came not to be served but to serve, and to give his life a ransom for many. (Mark 10:42b–45)

No slave can serve two masters; for a slave will either hate the one and love the other, or be devoted to the one and despise the other. You cannot serve God and wealth. (Luke 16:13)

Over the ages, Christians have often abused these and similar passages. Sometimes they have been used to give a divine stamp of approval to the institution of slavery—if Jesus used images of slavery, he must have thought it was OK for people to be slaves and slaveholders. At other times, they have been used to push for self-denial and even self-hatred as ends in themselves. But Christ only calls on us to deny ourselves so that we can serve him, follow him—and serve others who follow him. We give up the pursuit of wealth and status, not because they are evil, but so that we can concentrate our energy on pursuing holiness in Christ's service. He is the master whose exaltation is our work. Whether we are exalted or brought low in the course of serving him is unimportant.

One of the great examples of agreeing to God's will without consideration of status is Mary, the mother of Jesus. In response to the angel's confusing message, she could have said, "But I'm a good girl. If I'm discovered to be pregnant and unmarried, the least I have to worry about is losing my reputation. Joseph could refuse to take me as his wife, and my father could cast me out of my home. I could even be killed!" But instead her answer is, "Here I am, the servant of the Lord; let it be with me according to your word" (Luke 1:38). A few verses later, Mary sings a song expressing her confidence in a God who reverses the world's ideas of rank and status, who exalts the lowly and brings low the high and mighty:

> He has brought down the powerful from their thrones, and lifted up the lowly; he has filled the hungry with good things, and sent the rich away empty. (Luke 1:52–53)

Closer to our own time, we have a wonderful model of learning to accept all the changes of doing and suffering, being employed and laid aside, being exalted and brought low. She was born Marie-Françoise Thérèse Martin on January 2, 1873. When, at fifteen, she entered the Carmelite convent in Lisieux, she took the name Thérèse de L'Enfant Jésus et de la Sainte Face—Thérèse of the Child Jesus and of the Holy Face. Since her death on September 30, 1897, she has been known mostly as Thérèse de Lisieux.

Thérèse was only four when her mother died. She decided that her older sister Josephine could be a substitute, her "little mother." And so it seems only natural that when Josephine became a Carmelite (Thérèse was nine at the time), Thérèse would want to follow her. When Thérèse was fourteen, she began trying to enter the convent, even though the minimum age for entrance was twenty-one. With her father's cooperation, she worked her way up through the ecclesiastical hierarchy, seeking a dispensation. When the local bishop refused her, she even took her case to Pope Leo XIII! She and her father went to Rome as part of a tour group. When the group was given an audience with the pope—basically a receiving line—Thérèse broke protocol to ask for her dispensation. When the startled pope said that it would happen if it was God's will, Thérèse was ready to argue her case. Swiss Guards stepped in and escorted her out. But the permission arrived by the end of the next month, and a few months later she entered the convent.

How did a fifteen-year-old girl deal with the ups and downs of hopes raised and hopes dashed—with feeling exalted and being brought low again? She offered it all to Jesus for his amusement. In her auto-biography, after telling the story of her audience with Leo XIII, she wrote,

> For some time now, I had been offering myself to the Child Jesus as His little plaything, telling Him not to treat me as the sort of expensive toy that children only look at, without daring to touch. I wanted Him to treat me like a little ball, so value-less that it can be thrown on the ground, kicked about, pierced and left lying in a corner, or pressed close to His heart if He wants. In other words, I wished only to amuse the Child Jesus and let Him do with me exactly as He liked. Jesus had heard me, and in Rome He pierced His little plaything, because He wanted, I expect, to see what was inside; then, satisfied with what He found, He dropped His little ball and fell asleep. What did he dream about? What happened to the abandoned little ball?
>
> Jesus dreamed that He was still playing, that He kept picking up His little ball and throwing it down again, that He rolled it far from Him, but in the end, held it close to His heart, never to let it slip from His hands again. You can guess how sad the little ball was, left lying on the ground, though it went on hoping against hope.[1]

This dream is what Thérèse saw as Jesus' plan for her future. She might be bounced around a lot and seemingly forgotten, but she knew her destiny was to be loved and cherished by Jesus. And for a little ball, that's all that matters, because that is how toys become Real.[2]

Thérèse saw each moment as an opportunity to amuse the Child Jesus, to let Jesus delight in her. This attitude made each moment precious. It also allowed her to take her life lightly, to look at both good times and bad times with humor. It even helped her to put away hopes of being a missionary—she was much too sickly to handle such a job—and accept being a little nobody in a quiet convent. She wondered why some people should receive such great graces and do great things, while others were much less gifted—why some were exalted for God and others brought low.

> Jesus chose to enlighten me on this mystery. He opened the book of nature before me, and I saw that every flower He has created has a beauty of its own, that the splendor of the rose and the lily's whiteness do not deprive the violet of its scent nor make less ravishing the daisy's charm. I saw that if every little flower wished to be a rose, Nature would lose her spring adornments, and the fields would be no longer enameled with their varied flowers.[3]

Thérèse regularly referred to herself in her autobiography as a little flower, a metaphor so dominant that it became her nickname.

Though Thérèse saw herself as small and simple, her sister Pauline knew that others could benefit greatly by learning from her willingness to abandon herself so completely to God. And since Pauline had become Reverend Mother Agnès of God, the prioress of the convent, she could begin the process of introducing Thérèse to the world. First she made Thérèse the assistant to the novice mistress, so that she could help shape new arrivals in the convent. This was in 1893, only two years after Thérèse's final vows and shortly after her twentieth birthday. The next year, she ordered Thérèse to write the story of her life. She wrote about her childhood and her first years in the convent, putting down her memories in a cheap composition book. During the last year of her life, she was ordered to bring the story up to date. The last few pages were written in pencil because Thérèse had become too weak to manage the movement of dipping a pen. After Thérèse died, Mother Agnès edited and arranged publication of *The Story of a Soul*. Thérèse was canonized in 1921, and in 1998 she was the third woman to be declared a Doctor of the Church—one whose writings are commended as instructive for all Christians. Quite an exaltation for a simple young woman who died at 24! And although she named herself The Little Flower, Thérèse is depicted in religious art holding an armful of roses.

What, then, has this good Doctor taught me? Mostly I admire and try to learn from her ability to view both exaltation and being brought low with a dose of humor. That is, I try not to take myself too seriously. Of course, I fail regularly and get all bent out of shape over some imagined slight. Or, when a parishioner says that my sermon was just what she needed, I convince myself that it's because I'm a great preacher and forget about the Spirit's all-important role in both my speaking and her hearing. There are even times I still dream about being the famous pastor of a large, "high-steeple" church or a best-selling author being interviewed by Katie Couric. Usually I catch myself— or my wife punctures the balloon for me.

When I was reading the *Philokalia*, a collection of writings on the spiritual life by early Orthodox writers, I was struck by the negative things being said about self-esteem. Wasn't self-esteem important? Didn't Whitney Houston sing to us that "learning to love yourself is the greatest love of all"? Wasn't this the very sort of thing pointed to by folks who denounced traditional Christianity as psychologically unhealthy and life-denying? And then I figured out what the ancient writers were really talking about.

By self-esteem they meant an inaccurately positive self-image, the kind of pride that goes before a fall—or a puncture. They meant thinking that because you can fast four days while your neighbor can only last two, God must love you twice as much. They meant claiming all the credit when you use the gifts God has given you. They meant exalting yourself by putting others down. They meant tooting your own horn.

In contrast, humility is really an accurate self-image. Humility is not putting ourselves down or hating ourselves, but rather putting ourselves right where we belong—as God's (often fairly useless) servants. It's no accident that humor and humility get discussed so close together. Both come from the Latin *humus*—earth. And both involve a fairly earthy reality check, an unabashed look at how foolish we can be about ourselves and others. Teresa of Avila equates self-knowledge, humility, and walking in the truth. In *The Interior Castle* she wrote,

> Once I was pondering why our Lord was so fond of this virtue of humility, and this thought came to me. . . . It is because God is supreme Truth; and to be humble is to walk in truth, for it is a very deep truth that of ourselves we have nothing good but only misery and nothingness. Whoever does not understand this walks in falsehood. The more anyone understands it, the more he pleases the supreme Truth because he is walking in truth. [4]

Surely such self-knowledge also includes an appreciation of our God-given spiritual gifts and abilities—and the awareness of their source. If God has given us a beautiful singing voice or a special gift for comforting the sick or a talent for organizing church dinners, then refusing to use such abilities out of a false idea of self-denial is as arrogant as claiming for ourselves tasks for which we have no talent or training. Again, the truly important thing is that God be exalted, that Christ be lifted up. What happens to us in the process is much less significant. For we are no longer our own: we are God's.

Emptiness

I am no longer my own,
but thine.
Put me to what thou wilt,
rank me with whom thou wilt;
put me to doing, put me to suffering;
let me be employed for thee or laid aside for thee,
exalted for thee or
brought low for thee;

LET ME BE FULL, LET ME BE EMPTY;

let me have all things, let me have nothing;
I freely and heartily yield all things to thy
pleasure and disposal.
And now, O glorious and blessed God,
Father, Son, and Holy Spirit,
thou art mine, and I am thine.
So be it.
And the covenant which I have made
on earth, let it be ratified in heaven.
Amen.

CHAPTER 6

Emptiness

Let me be full, let me be empty.

WITH THIS CLAUSE the prayer shifts gears from talking about *doing* and *not doing* to looking at *having* and *not having*. I'd love to be able to tell you that when I hit this phrase in the Covenant Prayer I think about something deep, profound. But I don't—at least not at first. You see, I'm fat—not quite grotesque, but well beyond stocky—and usually on a diet. Even when I am not being diet-careful, I am diet-conscious. When I pray the Covenant prayer during my morning prayers, it is usually shortly after swigging down a tasty diet shake that leaves me neither full nor empty. So the first thing that comes to mind is my stomach and how I wish it were fuller but know it needs to be empty. I have even incorporated my desire to lose weight into my breath prayer: "More of you, Lord, less of me." Did the pun occur to you earlier when I mentioned the prayer? I really must decrease. My doctor tells me so.

Obviously, this approach to fullness and emptiness could be extended to other things in my life besides my stomach: my bookshelves, my house, my office, even my schedule. But the next phrase of the prayer is about having and not having things, so I'd like to defer the subject to the next chapter. There are other, deeper, meanings for this phrase to explore in this chapter, spiritual kinds of filling and emptying.

The place to start, then, is with the Holy Spirit. I really would like to be filled with the Spirit and, therefore, filled with love. Wouldn't you? After all, Christian spiritual formation is the process of learning to surrender ourselves to the Spirit's transforming power, so that we can be filled with God's love to the point where it overflows into the world. Or, as the hymn puts it, I want the Spirit of the living God to "melt me, mold me, fill me, use me."[1]

This kind of filling with the Spirit is what the early Methodists called going on to perfection. It is growing in love and in submission to God's will until we truly love God with all our heart and soul and mind and strength. It is being filled with the "love divine, all loves excelling." Another old hymn spells this out:

> Breathe on me, Breath of God,
>   fill me with life anew,
> That I may love what thou dost love,
>   and do what thou wouldst do.
>
> Breathe on me, Breath of God,
>   until my heart is pure,

Until with thee I will one will,
    to do and to endure.

Breathe on me, Breath of God,
    till I am wholly thine,
Till all this earthly part of me
    glows with thy fire divine.[2]

The problem with asking for this filling is that our hearts are already filled with other stuff, other loves. Some of these—the love of spouse, children, friends—are quite compatible with the love of God and can become part of that love. But others, grown out of control into idolatries of self (as in "Boy, he's sure full of himself!"), wealth, church, nation, need to be swept out. This is why the psalmist prays to be washed thoroughly from iniquity, cleansed from sin, and purged with hyssop before asking, "Create in me a clean heart, O God, and put a new and right spirit within me" (Psalm 51:10). And it is why Charles Wesley prays, "O that in me the sacred fire might now begin to glow; burn up the dross of base desire and make the mountains flow."[3] We have to be emptied out, swept clean, before we can be filled with the Spirit.

When I was around ten years old, my Dad and I went on the haunted house ride at a local amusement park. I was very excited as we rode in a little car that jerked us about in the darkness, and suddenly scary, brightly colored monsters seemed to leap at us. Then the ride stopped. We sat in the darkness for a while. Then bright work-lights came on, and someone shouted that the ride was broken and we'd have to walk out. Now I could see that the ride was just one big room with the track for the cars crisscrossing back and forth. Around the edges of the room were the "monsters," now revealed to be garishly painted papier-mâché over chicken wire. What had seemed exciting now just seemed cruddy.

So it is when the light of Christ shines in our hearts, when the wind and flame of the Spirit blow through. What once seemed exciting and special now seems cheap and tawdry. In John's Gospel we read:

> And this is the judgment, that the light has come into the world, and people loved darkness rather than light because their deeds were evil. For all who do evil hate the light and do not come into the light, so that their deeds may not be exposed. But those who do what is true come to the light, so that it may be clearly seen that their deeds have been done in God. (John 3:19–21)

So before we can pray, "Let me be full of the Spirit," we need to pray, "Let me be empty of everything within me that blocks the Spirit. Help me to stop doing the deeds of darkness. Help me to give up loves that get in the way of loving you. Melt and refine whatever can be transformed for your service and burn away all the dross that is left."

Even though it's helpful for discussion to separate the movements of emptying and filling, experience is not so compartmentalized. God doesn't wait for us to be completely cleansed before pouring the Spirit into us. God loves us as we are and doesn't wait for us to be worthy before showing that love. God will take any room we offer, even a crack. God is eager for us to experience God's love.

When I was in my first parish, I realized that I didn't know how to pray. Oh, I knew how to lead worship and write liturgical prayers. But I had never been taught what having a prayer life meant. So I started reading. I read books on prayer, worked through workbooks, sampled the spiritual classics. I tried various methods of prayer, including praying the Jesus Prayer when I was walking alone or when I had to wait alone. Then it happened. I was at a Pastors' School at Albright College, sitting alone at a desk in a mostly darkened dorm room and reading *The Practice of the Presence of God* by Brother Lawrence. My roommate was at a worship service, but I was tired and had hay fever and stayed behind. Suddenly I felt as if someone had come up behind me and had given me a big bear hug. It was my first really vivid and direct experience of God's presence and God's love. It only lasted a moment, but made a great difference, the difference between knowing about God's love and knowing God.

When my roommate returned and I told him what had happened, he said, "I don't know what to say to someone whose heart has been strangely warmed." He was referring to the famous experience of John Wesley at a Moravian meeting in Aldersgate Street in London. Wesley described it as a moment of assurance, of knowing that the general truth that Christ died for sinners applied to him, personally, and that *he* was forgiven. Or, to put it in the terms of this chapter, it was a moment of feeling filled with the love and forgiveness that had previously only been known theoretically, intellectually. Along with that feeling had come a new spiritual power to resist temptation, a lasting effect. Wesley knew that this experience was the beginning of a process of emptying and filling that would continue the rest of his life.

But even when that process is well under way, there is another kind of filling and emptying that may just be starting. Spiritual writers have traditionally spoken of the spiritual journey as a three-fold path. The first part of the journey is purgation, the cleansing we've talking about. The second part of the journey is illumination, a time of being filled with a sense of God's presence and God's love. This is a time when prayer seems to flow easily, when we find it easy to meditate on Scripture and to reflect on verbal prayers. Although purgation continues, this growing ease and comfort in prayer, this more vivid experience of God's loving presence, distinguish this part of the journey. The third part of the journey is union, being joined so closely to God that we can lose ourselves in God's love, that our will is united to God's will. At least that's what the mystics say. I haven't walked that far on the path, yet.

Between the second and third parts is an interlude, a new and deeper time of emptying. John of the Cross calls this the dark night of the soul. He describes it as a time of spiritual desolation. Old and comfortable ways of praying suddenly fall flat. We can't concentrate on meditations or other prayers. The sense of God's presence lessens or disappears. John writes, "God . . . leaves the intellect in darkness, the will in aridity, the memory in emptiness, and the affections in supreme affliction, bitterness, and anguish by depriving the soul of the feeling and satisfaction it previously obtained from spiritual blessings."[4] It seems that God has abandoned us or is punishing us. Other periods of spiritual dryness seem lush by comparison. This, says John, is purgative contemplation, when the soul "feels very vividly indeed the shadow of death, the sighs of death, and the sorrows of hell, all of which reflect the feeling of God's absence, of being chastised and rejected by him, and of being unworthy of him, as well as the object of his anger."[5]

And yet, John sees this as a time of invitation, not of punishment. God is inviting us to surrender even our attachment to God's blessings. Why? Because we can get so caught up in enjoying the feelings of reassurance, love, forgiveness, and closeness that we begin to pray in order to get the feelings and not to be closer to God. We can become blessing junkies, eager for our next fix of prayer. And when suddenly the fix doesn't work any more, we have a chance to offer God purer prayer, to love God for God's own sake and not for the blessings. We are emptied of all natural feelings and affections so that we can be open to spiritual union with God. John explains,

> Oh, what a sheer grace it is for the soul to be freed from the house of its senses! This good fortune, in my opinion, can only be understood by the ones who have tasted it. For then such persons will become clearly aware of the wretched servitude and the many miseries they suffered when they were subject to the activity of their faculties and appetites. They will understand how the life of the spirit is true freedom and wealth and embodies inestimable goods.[6]

Earlier we looked at Thomas Green's image of contemplative prayer as floating. He applies this image to the idea of the dark night:

> The whole experience of the dark night or the cloud of unknowing appears to be the Lord's way of trying

to make floaters out of swimmers. . . . He wants us to have as *our* goal our total surrender to the flow of this tide. He has another goal, it is true. . . . He is leading us somewhere. . . . He would like us to trust him enough to relax, to leave the goal wholly to him, and to concretize our trust by savoring fully the expanse of sky and sea which is open to our gaze now. Only those who are totally secure in their love can live thus fully the present moment.[7]

Once again, God has a plan for us. God doesn't take away the consolations of meditation to leave us desolate, wondering why our swimming doesn't seem to get us anywhere. God empties us so that we can be filled.

Our spiritual life involves many periods of being filled and being emptied. Sometimes we need to enjoy the comforts of this life; at others we need to let them go. Sometimes God calls us to purgation, to emptying out the crud clogging our hearts; at other times God fills us with a more vivid experience of the Holy Spirit, a greater awareness of the Spirit working in us and through us. Sometimes God blesses us with a sense of God's presence; at others our spiritual life is empty and dry. All these times are part of our spiritual journey, and God knows best what we need next. And so we pray, "Let me be full, let me be empty." The rhythm and balance of the two are up to God.

Addictions

I am no longer my own,
but thine.
Put me to what thou wilt,
rank me with whom thou wilt;
put me to doing, put me to suffering;
let me be employed for thee or laid aside for thee,
exalted for thee or
brought low for thee;
let me be full, let me be empty;
LET ME HAVE ALL THINGS,
LET ME HAVE NOTHING;
I freely and heartily yield all things to thy
pleasure and disposal.
And now, O glorious and blessed God,
Father, Son, and Holy Spirit,
thou art mine, and I am thine.
So be it.
And the covenant which I have made
on earth, let it be ratified in heaven.
Amen.

CHAPTER 7

Addictions

Let me have all things, let me have nothing.

FROM THE ETHEREAL WORLD of purgation, spiritual blessings, and devastating desolations, the prayer brings us back to the earthy world of things, of stuff. Here is yet another kind of detachment. The prayer reminds us that we are not defined by the stuff we have, any more than we are defined by our jobs or our status or even the blessings we receive when we pray. It shouldn't really matter whether we're rich or poor, whether we have lots of stuff or lose it all. And I understand that, at least in theory. What I have or how much I have doesn't determine my relation with God. God loves me, not my stuff.

Still, whenever I turn on the television or open the newspaper or a magazine, I am bombarded with messages from folks determined to convince me that my life is empty—or at least diminished—if I don't buy the stuff they want to sell me. They all claim that my stuff does define me. The clothes make the man. You are what you eat. If you want to be sophisticated, with it, then of course you need to see this movie, read this book. You must see this television show or you'll feel stupid, out of the loop, when your friends are all talking about it.

Some of the time these appeals wash right over me. I don't feel a great need to be sexually attractive. Or at least I know that what car I drive or what clothes I wear are not the key to maintaining and building my relationship with my wife. So I can get along just fine with my cheap little Hyundai and my second-hand clergy shirts. I don't buy things simply because they are status symbols, that is, because having them shows that I am wealthy enough to afford them. Traditional luxury items don't really do much for me.

But then there are books. There are always reasons to buy a new book. There are dozens of books on spirituality and preaching and Bible criticism published every year. Isn't it my responsibility as a pastor and writer on spiritual subjects to keep up with the flow, to keep current? And sometimes I see a book that seems to be the kind of book I'd really like to see published, even if I may not have time to read it. How can I encourage the publisher to print more books like that, other than by buying this one? It's not really wasting money on a book I may never read. It's investing in the future of religious publishing. And then I spot a fantasy novel that's the next installment in a series. I already have the first five, so surely it's only right to keep going with number six. And so it goes.

Once a monk asked his abbot what was the matter with owning just a book or two. How could that destroy the ideal of poverty? And the abbot explained that if he owned a book, then he'd want a shelf to put it on. And then he'd want a door on his cell to protect it. And soon the whole community would be fragmented. At this point I need several shelves just to hold the books I haven't read, but haven't given up hope of reading. And my wife and I need a large house and two offices to hold all the books we own. And, of course, there were good reasons for buying each one. At least, I thought there were at the time. And it's a curious thing that I seem to do better at keeping up with my purchases of science fiction, fantasy, and mysteries than I do with all my serious, work-related purchases.

Computers are another problem area for me. Isn't it obvious that I'll have a much easier time writing if I have a powerful new computer running the latest software and with a built-in CD-ROM drive to play music while I write, than if I'm limping along on a six-year old machine running a ten-year-old word processor (practically a historical curiosity in computer terms)? Of course, the fact that I can't even think of purchasing the latest games without the latest hardware hardly matters. At least, not right now. I only have time to play short games, not the great epics I used to enjoy. And should I ever get some time to tackle a really big game, I have several I bought soon after getting my current computer that I've never finished—some I've never even played.

The truth is, there are always arguments to justify accumulating more stuff, regardless of whether we really need it or not. The problem is that the more stuff we have, the more time we have to spend taking care of it, and the less time we have to spend in prayer or serving God. I find myself becoming a servant of my stuff. At the very least, my life becomes more and more complicated. I have to devote more and more space to storing my stuff, and more and more time searching through it to find just what I wanted. But of course, as soon as I sell some of my stuff, I find I've sold the very book I wanted to consult. I have a long way to go in simplifying my life. But through it all, the Covenant Prayer holds an ideal of detachment in front of me: "Let me have all things, let me have nothing." It keeps me aware of my greed, my desire to have all things— or at least an awful lot of things in certain categories.

The Covenant Prayer can also remind us of the example of folks who got along very well with pretty close to nothing.

- There's Antony, the first of the Desert Fathers. He left the temptations of civilization to go to a cave out in the Egyptian desert, where he wrestled with demons and lived on hard bread that could be stored for months.

- There's young Francis of Assisi, who gave up all

possessions, even handing his father the clothes he was wearing. Then, dressed in a simple robe, he spent his days rebuilding a falling-down church and his evenings begging for food from former neighbors.

- There's Carlo Carretto, who left the busyness of being a church executive to live among the poor of North Africa, making his tire-tread sandals.

And, much closer to home, there's John Woolman, a Quaker tailor from New Jersey, who lived in the period just before the Revolutionary War. Unlike the others, Woolman lived "in the world." He had a wife and family and his own home. He had his own business, making clothes and selling cloth and notions. But Woolman was also a man with a holy mission. He spent his spare time traveling throughout the American colonies (usually on foot!) speaking to individual Quakers and to Quaker meetings, urging folks to give up owning slaves. When his business grew to where it began to interfere with this mission, he decided to prune it. He even encouraged customers to go to his competition. So he managed to cut it back to where it provided for his needs but didn't take over his life. We can dismiss Antony, Francis, and Carlo as special cases, folks called to lives of radical poverty. But Woolman's example of simplicity is harder to wave away, particularly when reinforced by the continuing witness of other Quakers, such as Richard J. Foster, who wrote *Freedom of Simplicity*. And where I live in central Pennsylvania, it's just a short drive for me to see the living witness of the Amish.

I could certainly simplify my life a lot. At least I think I could. It's just that I've grown so attached to my stuff, my busyness, my diversions. And when I look at them more closely, I can see that these attachments are outward signs of deeper addictions, needs that become insistent cravings. The things to which we remain attached tell us about the needs we still seek to satisfy through things rather than through God.

One is the need for input. If we are bombarded from the outside, from television, movies, books, then we don't have to spend time alone with ourselves. There's no chance to brood if our minds are kept busy with other diversions, however trivial. The problem is that the stream of input closes off other possibilities, too. In his book *The Other Side of Silence* Morton Kelsey has a long meditation on the Soul Room. He pictures it as a small apartment where television and radio are blaring simultaneously just for the sake of distraction. Why?

> We are afraid of our own company. . . we fear that we cannot stand ourselves and our own nothing-ness. . . . We are afraid of our helplessness . . . bet-ter to hurry and do something than to be still and face our helplessness before the god of the market-place. . . THE PAIN OF NOT BEING GOD!

We are afraid of the pain that has been locked deep in our hearts, hidden under books and piles of clothing and china and useless things . . . we are afraid of our failures, follies, our sins . . . the monsters of our desires and feelings . . . the old beast within us, the old angry ego that wills never to give in.[1]

But when the distracting television and radio are turned off, says Kelsey, we can hear a faint knocking: Christ waiting patiently to be invited in. How much better would we be at hearing Christ's call if we spent less time paying attention to the world? How would our lives change if our reading took us deeper into a few carefully chosen classics rather than constantly rushing through the latest best sellers?

Another great craving I have is for accomplishment. And face it, that's a tough one for pastors. Sure, we can pat ourselves on the back for getting a sermon written, a bulletin run off, a member visited in the hospital, a statistical report completed. But even when we've finished one of those, we can't be sure if we've really accomplished anything, or if we're just spinning our wheels. We can't measure our impact in people's lives. We hardly ever get concrete feedback about whether our efforts have helped someone to grow closer to God in Christ. And some of our efforts may simply be planting seeds that will take years to grow and bear fruit. It can seem that we try and try and get nowhere. There's a story about a pastor who went out every evening to watch the freight train roll through town. When asked why, he answered, "It's the only thing that moves in this town without me pushing it."

But there is one area of my life where I can get instant feedback and a definite win or loss: computer games. In about five minutes I either win FreeCell or run into a dead end. If I win (about 79% of the time!), that's great. And if I lose, I can try again or go back and learn where I went wrong. So when the craving gets too bad and I need an accomplishment fix, I can surely fit in one quick game. And another. And another. And soon an hour has gone by, and I realize that, however good I may feel about my game-playing abilities, I'm not getting my book written or my sermon preparation done. I might even be running late for a meeting, or the clock might have magically jumped from a little before bedtime to well after. Sometimes the computer game habit that soothes my accomplishment addiction can be a real problem.

Of course, it's not the computer that's to blame here. There are many ways other than computer games to get an instant accomplishment fix. When I was in college, I played bridge for hours when I was feeling sociable, and solitaire (with real cards in those dark ages before home computers) when I wasn't. At other times I've turned to crossword puzzles or other word games. Other people knit or whittle. The addiction is the same: to seeing results that let us know clearly whether we've succeeded or failed in a short time.

I realize that I've been talking a lot about my own addictions and the underlying need for input and accomplishment. That's because I know them. I've spent time embracing them and time resisting them. Your addictions may be quite different. You may seek ways to deaden feeling with alcohol or other depressants or to heighten it through the adrenalin rush of driving too fast or living "on the edge." You may collect things—teddy bears, hubcaps, objets d'art—the way I collect the second-hand experiences I get through movies and books. Maybe you fill your days with work and your nights with parties so you never have to be alone. We have all formed habits that are our own personal ways of avoiding the pain of not being God. One way or another, we are all addicts.

Like most addicts, I tell myself I can quit anytime I really want to. After all, I have given up computer games for Lent a couple of times now. But the Covenant Prayer calls us to a different approach. Not just to change the surface behavior, but to surrender the underlying craving. We don't really need to worry about whether we're accomplishing great things for Christ. What we do need is to follow faithfully, to be about the work he has given us to do, and to leave the end result to him. If I could truly arrive at this kind of surrender, I might not crave the accomplishment fix of games or need distraction from brooding about whether anything I do makes a real difference. If you could truly arrive at this kind of surrender, you might be able to let go of the underlying needs that fuel your addictions. We wouldn't be so dependent on things to comfort us and distract us and reassure us about who we are. Whether we had all things or nothing truly wouldn't matter. When we stop to think about it, we know the problem, and the Covenant Prayer offers a radical solution, that is, one that goes to the root. What holds us back?

Now here's some really good news. It's not all up to us. God works with us. We can actively try to detach ourselves from the things we have used as props for our egos, to loosen our grip on our stuff. But at the same time, God can work to pry our fingers loose. The consolations I spoke of in the last chapter are God's temporary tools to help us let go of things and grab hold of God. They serve as a bridge, a reminder that while all sorts of things can give us a temporary rush, nothing—no thing—can be ultimately fulfilling. Fancy foods lose their savor, and books leave us bored. We come out of a roller coaster ride or a blockbuster movie wondering, "Is that all?" Even our greatest accomplishments seem as trivial as winning a computer game. This is another kind of dark night, what John of the Cross calls the active night of the senses—active because our beginning to turn to God in prayer is what makes it possible.[2] As our will becomes increasingly fixed on God—as we surrender ourselves in abandonment— we realize that only God's love can truly fill us, truly satisfy our longings. As Jesus says to the woman at the well, "Those who drink of the water that I will give them will never be thirsty. The water that I will give will become in them a spring of water gushing up to eternal life" (John 4:14). And our response (to paraphrase the woman) is, "Lord, give me this water, and I won't have to keep looking for substitutes." For if we have this one thing, it really doesn't matter whether we have all else or nothing else.

Yielding Everything

I am no longer my own,
but thine.
Put me to what thou wilt,
rank me with whom thou wilt;
put me to doing, put me to suffering;
let me be employed for thee or laid aside for thee,
exalted for thee or
brought low for thee;
let me be full, let me be empty;
let me have all things, let me have nothing;
**I FREELY AND HEARTILY
YIELD ALL THINGS
TO THY PLEASURE AND DISPOSAL.**
And now, O glorious and blessed God,
Father, Son, and Holy Spirit,
thou art mine, and I am thine.
So be it.
And the covenant which I have made
on earth, let it be ratified in heaven.
Amen.

CHAPTER 8

Yielding Everything

*I freely and heartily yield all things
to thy pleasure and disposal.*

HERE, NEAR THE END OF THE PRAYER, we are brought back to the question with which we started. Will we yield, surrender, resign all things to God's control? Or will we hold back? Will we trust God's guidance and seek to do God's will? Will we continue to trust only in ourselves? Or will we yield ourselves to some human leader or some human-made institution? What's it going to be?

As I indicated way back in the Introduction, we can push behind this question to one even more fundamental or foundational. Is God trustworthy? Is God for us? Adrian van Kaam (using the term "mystery of formation" rather than "God") calls this the foundational formation decision:

> Is this mystery of formation meaningful and beneficial? Can we abandon our lives to this mysterious process in a movement of seminal faith, hope, and consonance? . . .

Every person decides whether to believe and trust in the meaningfulness of the ongoing formation of life and world. No matter what we decide, this primordial option and subsequent disposition will profoundly color our formation history.[1]

If we answer this fundamental question affirmatively, then it would follow that we would want to align ourselves as closely as possible with this mysterious force that gives meaning and purpose to all of life. That is, saying *Yes* to God means setting ourselves on the road to complete abandonment. Note that even if we say *No*, our spirits will continue to be formed, both by the world around us (often urging us continue our negative decision) and by God, who never gives up on us. But until we say *Yes*, we are much more likely to be deformed, shaped in ways that lead us further from God's loving plan for us. (For more on the process of spiritual formation, see Appendix B.)

The call to complete surrender, to self-abandonment, has been put in many ways. Jesus says, "If any want to become my followers, let them deny themselves and take up their cross and follow me" (Mark 8:34). Paul says,

> I appeal to you therefore, brothers and sisters, by the mercies of God, to present your bodies as a living sacrifice, holy and acceptable to God, which is your spiritual worship. Do not be conformed to this

world, but be transformed by the renewing of your minds, so that you may discern what is the will of God—what is good and acceptable and perfect. (Romans 12:1–2)

Abandonment means the surrender of our will to God's will, as well as detachment from anything that is not God. There is no such thing as "good enough" abandonment. God will keep calling us onward to complete self-surrender, to complete transformation. Jean-Pierre de Caussade writes,

> No matter what it is we attach ourselves to, God will step in and upset our plans so that, instead of peace, we shall find ourselves in the midst of confusion, trouble and folly. As soon as we say, "I must go this way, I must consult this person, I must act like this," God at once says the opposite and withdraws his power from those means which we ourselves have chosen. So we discover the emptiness of all created things, are forced to turn to God and be content with him.[2]

John Sammis says the same thing more poetically in his hymn "Trust and Obey":

> But we never can prove
> The delights of his love
> Until all on the altar we lay;
> For the favor he shows,

For the joy he bestows,
Are for them who will trust and obey.[3]

Whenever I sing this hymn, I think of a series of scenes in Hannah Hurnard's allegorical novel, *Hind's Feet in High Places*. The book tells the story of Much-Afraid and her long journey to leave her village of Much-Trembling and go to live with the Shepherd in the High Places. At several points along the way, Much-Afraid stops to build an altar and lay upon it another aspect of her life. The first altar is for "her trembling, rebelling will."

> A little spurt of flame came from somewhere, and in an instant nothing but a heap of ashes was lying on the altar. That is to say, she thought at first there were only ashes, but the Shepherd told her to look closer, and there among the ashes she saw a little stone of some kind, a dark-colored, common-looking pebble.
>
> "Pick it up and take it with you," said the Shepherd gently, "as a memorial of this altar which you built, and all that it stands for."[4]

This is only the first of many altars at which Much-Afraid surrenders more and more of herself until all that remains is "the flame of concentrated desire to do his will. Everything else had died down and fallen into ashes."[5]

"I freely and heartily yield all things . . ." Not just some things. This isn't a negotiation with God, where I agree to yield in some areas, but reserve others for myself. It's not like a major league sports expansion draft, where the owner of an established team can say, "You can pick any of my players except A, B, and C." When we yield our wills to God, we must surrender everything else.

But that's not the end of the story. God may give back to us some of the things we give up, so that we can cherish them on God's behalf. This is the true meaning of stewardship. God entrusts us with people to love, tasks to perform, things to care for. At the very least, God gives us ourselves to love and cherish, not as we were, but transformed and new in God's grace. But God will probably entrust us with much more than that.

John Wesley's sermon "The Use of Money" has three main points that are often quoted: gain all you can, save all you can, and give all you can. But often folks ignore what that last point really means. I sing in a barbershop chorus and when our effort seems half-hearted, our director often asks us, "Come on boys, how much can you give me?" And the answer we shout back is, "All of it!" In his sermon, Wesley explains that "give all you can" really means "give all":

> If you desire to be a faithful and a wise steward out
> of that portion of your Lord's goods which he has

for the present lodged in your hands but with the right of resuming whenever it pleases him, first, provide things needful for your self: food to eat, raiment to put on, whatever nature moderately requires for preserving the body in health and strength. Secondly, provide these for your wife, your children, your servants, or any others who pertain to your household. If, when this is done, there be an overplus left, then "do good to them that are of the household of faith." If there be an overplus still, "as you have opportunity, do good unto all men." In so doing, you give all you can; nay, in a sound sense, all you have: for all that is laid out in this manner is really given to God.[6]

It takes a while for us to grow to the point where we can indeed yield all things to God, let alone love them and use them only for God's sake. Nearly eight and a half centuries ago, Bernard of Clairvaux, the abbot of a Cistercian monastery, was asked to write about why and how we should love God. His response, a short treatise "On Loving God," speaks of four degrees of love—stages we all pass through.

The first degree of love is loving ourselves for our own sake. That is, we are strictly looking out for ourselves, grabbing for all the gusto we can find in worldly things. Bernard says we are foolishly seeking "consumption, not consummation."[7] In essence, this is the time when we insist, "I am my own, and God can take a flying leap."

The second degree of love is loving God for our sake. We love God because of the wonderful things God does for us. We love God because loving God is supposed to get us goodies, blessings, warm happy feelings. This is a very functional, utilitarian kind of love. It is a gold-digger's practical love, not for our Father in heaven, but for our Sugar Daddy in the sky. And it may be the kind of love for God felt by many who call themselves Christians. At this stage we may say, "I am still my own, but I'm thankful for the things God does for me."

The third degree of love is loving God for God's sake. Having gotten to know God, having tasted the sweetness of God's love for us, "leads us to love God in purity more than our need alone would prompt us to do." This degree of love is captured in the hymn, "My God, I Love Thee":

> My God, I love thee, not because I hope for heaven thereby,
> Nor yet because, if I love not, I must forever die.
>
> Thou, O my Jesus, thou didst me upon the cross embrace;
> For me didst bear the nails and spear and manifold disgrace.
>
> Then why, O blessed Jesus Christ, should I not love thee
>   well?
> Not for the sake of winning heaven, nor of escaping hell.

Not with the hope of gaining aught, not seeking a reward,
But as thyself hast loved me, O everlasting Lord.

So would I love thee, dearest Lord, and in thy praise will sing;
Because thou art my loving God and my eternal King.[8]

This, at last, is when we can say, "I am no longer my own, but thine," not just because we think we should, but because we freely offer ourselves to God.

In Hurnard's story, the last thing Much-Afraid must lay on an altar is her natural love of the Shepherd (the second degree love). It has carried her far. But now she must pluck it out of her heart and offer it to God. She finds she cannot do this alone, but asks for and receives help. Once this love has been torn from her, though, she learns that "it was ripe for removal, the time had come."[9] She is ready to move on to the purer love of the third degree. "A sense of utter, overwhelming peace engulfed Much-Afraid. At last, the offering had been made and there was nothing left to be done."

The fourth degree of love, according to Bernard, is loving ourselves for God's sake. This really is being so completely united to God that loving God is loving ourselves in a love that overflows to all the world around us. Bernard notes,

To love in this ways is to become like God. As a drop of water seems to disappear completely in a quantity of wine, taking the wine's flavor and color; as red-hot iron becomes indistinguishable from the glow of fire and its own original form disappears; as air suffused with the light of the sun seems transformed into the brightness of the light, as if it were itself light rather than merely lit up; so, in those who are holy it is necessary for human affection to dissolve in some ineffable way, and be poured into the will of God. . . . The substance remains, but in another form, with another glory, another power.[10]

This is what Paul meant when he wrote, "It is no longer I who live, but it is Christ who lives in me. And the life I now live in the flesh I live by faith in the Son of God, who loved me and gave himself for me" (Galatians 2:20). Maybe Whitney Houston was right after all. Learning to love yourself—for God's sake—really is the greatest love of all. At least, it causes Bernard to shout for joy, "O holy and chaste love! O sweet and tender affection! O pure and sinless intention of the will—the more pure and sinless in that there is no mixture of self-will in it, the more sweet and tender in that everything it feels is divine."[11]

In a letter attached to the treatise, Bernard goes over the first three loves from a different angle: why we praise God. If we praise God's power, he says, then we act out of fear and are only slaves. If we praise the good things God has done for us, then we act out of greed and are mercenaries, hirelings. But if we praise God simply because God is good, then we are like children loving and honoring their father. Bernard says, "Neither fear nor love of self can convert the soul. They change the appearance of one's deed from time to time, but never one's character."[12] Only the love that grows through experiencing God's goodness can truly make us willing to surrender ourselves more and more until we have freely and heartily yielded all things to God's pleasure and disposal.

By now you may have realized that every time I pray this line, I am lying. Or at least I am making a gross overstatement. I know that my abandonment is far from complete, that much of my life still needs to be surrendered to God's pleasure and disposal. I am all too aware of my shortcomings, my problems. This awareness is not just a matter of being a pessimist who sees the glass as half empty; it goes back to John of the Cross's image of the soul as a window for God's light. If we are looking at the window, we quickly become aware of every speck, smear, or scratch. When we look at ourselves, it is much easier to focus on the flaws than to notice whatever light may pass through. Only others can see that.

When Bernard of Clairvaux set out to write a treatise on the steps of humility (as listed in the Rule of St. Benedict), he admitted, "I feared that it would be beyond me."[13] But, he said, he did know about the steps that lead to increasing pride, which he listed by more or less standing Benedict's list on its head. Similarly, while it may be hard to look directly at how close we have come to full surrender to God, it is easier to look at the ways in which we still cling to having our own way and to doing our own thing. Alleine set out a list of such ways, which he called the Devil's Ten Commandments. Here is that list, abridged and modernized. I suggest you spend some time with it. Where do you see yourself, hear echoes of your thoughts? Are there even places where you can't see why Alleine thought the idea was devilish? Where do you need to work on being no longer your own, but God's, on freely and heartily surrendering?

1. Live for yourself and mind your own business. This is the first and great commandment on which all the rest hang.

2. Let your will be your law. You are your own. Your tongue, time, and property are your own to do with as you will.

3. Make the best of the present time and of present things. Don't trade what you have for what you may have. Eat, drink and be merry, for tomorrow you may die. Make hay while the sun shines.

4. Stand fast in your freedom. Don't be a voluntary slave to a strict and restrained life.

5. Continue in sin, because grace has abounded. Christ died for sinners. God is merciful. Why then should you fear to do what you will?

6. Do as others do. Go along with the crowd and don't stand out. Why think you know better than others?

7. Do no more in religion than you must. Don't go overboard being righteous. A little faith, a little repentance will do fine.

8. Don't worry about small offenses. Thoughts are free and words are cheap. Who doesn't sin? Why fuss about your sins? Aren't they just little ones?

9. Don't be in a hurry. There's plenty of time to repent. When you are old, you'll have little else to do. Don't be old while you're young.

10. Trust God's mercy, rather than human tolerance. Better to sin than get in trouble with people. Don't stick your neck out.[14]

I am still bound in many ways by old habits and worldly responsibilities. So any yielding I do is not quite "freely." And since I continue to hold back in some areas of my life, the "heartily" should probably be "halfheartedly." But I want this part of the Covenant Prayer to be true. I want to grow to the point where I do freely and heartily yield all things to God. I am learning to love God for God's sake alone. So I am reluctant to settle for praying the truth: that in partial freedom and with some reservations I yield some things. The Covenant Prayer continues to serve as a goad, driving me onward.

In Conclusion

the covenant prayer

I am no longer my own, but thine.
Put me to what thou wilt,
rank me with whom thou wilt;
put me to doing, put me to suffering;
let me be employed for thee or laid aside for thee,
exalted for thee or
brought low for thee;
let me be full, let me be empty;
let me have all things, let me have nothing;
I freely and heartily yield all things to thy
pleasure and disposal.

**AND NOW, O GLORIOUS AND BLESSED
GOD, FATHER, SON, AND HOLY SPIRIT,
THOU ART MINE, AND I AM THINE.
SO BE IT.
AND THE COVENANT WHICH
I HAVE MADE ON EARTH,
LET IT BE RATIFIED IN HEAVEN.**

Amen.

CHAPTER 9

In Conclusion

And now, O glorious and blessed God,
Father, Son, and Holy Spirit,
thou art mine and I am thine. So be it.
And the covenant which I have made on earth,
let it be ratified in heaven.

WE COME TO THE END OF THE PRAYER with these final sentences. There's not a whole lot left to be said, but I would like to lift up three aspects of this conclusion.

The first aspect is doxology, literally a "word of glory" about God. Everyone knows that the Doxology comes after the offering in the worship service. So it seems only right that, after offering ourselves to God in so many ways through the body of the prayer, we sign off by praising God's glory. In fact, Christians are pretty enthusiastic about putting doxologies everywhere. The Lord's Prayer as given in Matthew's Gospel finishes with "deliver us from evil." But by no later than the beginning of the second century, Christians had added "for yours is the power and the glory forever."[1] I don't know when "the kingdom" got added. A few centuries later, Christians created the *Gloria Patri* ("Glory be to the Father. . . .") as a sort of Trinitarian postscript for the psalms. We just can't pray for very long without stopping to praise God.

A doxology may be particularly appropriate here at the end of the Covenant Prayer. In many lines the only pronoun is "me," so it's good to stop for a moment and remember that the other person, the thou/thee/thy of the prayer, is God almighty: Father, Son, and Holy Spirit. There are days when the rest of the prayer sort of slips past. But I almost always stop at the word glorious. It reminds me of the benediction I pronounce each Sunday, which begins, "And now go forth and give God the glory. . . ." That's the whole point of human existence. The author of Ephesians reminds us that all God has done for us in Christ is so that we "might live for the praise of his glory" (Ephesians 1:12). In the Westminster Shorter Catechism, the first question, "What is the chief end of man?" is to be answered, "Man's chief end is to glorify God, and to enjoy Him for ever."[2] So even in the midst of praising God, the Covenant Prayer reminds us that nothing is as important as glorifying God and enjoying life in God's presence.

The second aspect I'd like to lift up is the phrase, "Thou art mine and I am thine." Most of the Covenant Prayer is our explanation of how thoroughly we want to be God's—specifically, God's servants. But at least for a moment the prayer expresses another longing, to go beyond servanthood to intimacy. Joseph Alleine spelled this out more explicitly in the section of his covenant prayer that is the source for this phrase: " . . . thou art now become my covenant friend; and I through thine infinite grace am become thy covenant servant."[3] Now, to some extent, this reflects the language of the medieval feudal system, where the lord is called friend and bene-factor to the knight or serf who is bound to the lord's service. But it also taps into the promise of Jesus in John 15:15: "I do not call you servants any longer, because the servant does not know what the master is doing; but I have called you friends, because I have made known to you everything that I have heard from my Father." As we grow from knowing about God to knowing God, so we grow from being servants of Christ to being his friends. Or, as others put it, we grow from being slaves of God to being children of God.

This longing for intimacy with God is something that has already come up several times in the course of these reflections on the Covenant Prayer. It is why the "holy hug" at Albright was so important to me. It came out in my alternative ending to the dark cave medita-tion. It is the key image of Psalm 131: resting in God like a toddler in Mommy's lap. One of my favorite ways to seek inner silence is to picture myself sitting on a river bank leaning against Jesus, not doing or saying any-thing, but just watching the river together. Stray thoughts become logs floating in the river, but I just let them drift on by and pay attention only to the river and the sense of Christ's presence with me.

Writers on the spiritual life—especially the Carmelites, Teresa, John, and Thérèse—talk about intimacy with God in terms of spiritual marriage. The poetry of John of the Cross is full of the language of love, even in talking about the dark night:

> O guiding night!
> O night more lovely than the dawn!
> O night that has united
> the Lover with his beloved,
> transforming the beloved in her Lover.
>
> Upon my flowering breast,
> which I kept wholly for him alone
> there he lay sleeping,
> and I caressing him
> there in a breeze from the fanning cedars.[4]

Such intimacy seems far beyond my own experience. But I long to keep growing from being friend to being beloved. I would like to hear God say to me, "This is my beloved child, with whom I am well pleased." Or to be able to say with the Bride of the Song of Songs, "My beloved is mine and I am his" (Song of Solomon 2:16).

There is one final phrase worth lifting up for special attention: "Let it be ratified in heaven." It is one final reminder of how completely dependent we are on God's grace. We can make the brave resolutions of the

Covenant Prayer to surrender all control to God. But we cannot keep them without God's constant support. We can no more grit our teeth to make things so by sheer will power here, than in any other aspect of our lives. As Bernard of Clairvaux says, "Lord, you are good to the soul which seeks you. . . . But this is the most wonderful thing, that no one can seek you who has not already found you. . . . It is certain that every prayer which is not inspired is half-hearted."[5] Our self-abandonment is a growing cooperation with God, as bit by bit, God gives us the ability to surrender more and more to God.

We can be confident that this covenant of total surrender is indeed what God wants. We have seen how the call to self-abandonment can be found again and again in many different ways in the Bible and in spiritual classics. We can trust that God will indeed ratify in heaven the covenant we have made—that God will cooperate with our struggle to give ourselves completely to God.

When I grow discouraged about the slow pace of grace, about how many areas of my life need major work despite years of praying the Covenant Prayer, there is no phrase I pray more fervently than this plea for God's ratification. Here's what I want to do. I truly believe that it is what you want me to do, too. Heaven help me!

A Last Word

I HOPE THAT YOU HAVE FOUND this journey through the Covenant Prayer helpful, maybe even inspiring. It certainly has helped me to clarify some of my own thoughts and associations with the prayer. It has forced me to look closely at patterns I've been trying to break and the excuses I've made for holding back. And it has given me an excuse to revisit many old friends among the writers of spiritual classics.

It would be nice if reading this book helped you decide to make the Covenant Prayer a regular part of your spiritual life. But there are two even more important ways that I hope this book can have an impact in your life. The first is that you begin to pay more attention to the prayers you already pray, whether the Lord's Prayer, table grace, or any other regular verbal prayer. Think about what you're really saying to God. Listen to what God says to you through your praying. Consider how that prayer connects to other things you've learned about God, about living as a Christian, about spiritual formation. Second, I hope you've met someone—Teresa, Thérèse, John Woolman, Bernard, Carlo Carretto—you'd like to know a little better. They're all fascinating folks and their writings are readily available. If reading this book helps get you hooked on the classics, then I'll be happy and you'll be blessed.

A Brief History

THE COVENANT PRAYER as I learned it is not very old. It was redacted from older versions for a British Methodist prayer book in 1936. But its roots go deep in Methodism, and before that in the writings of two Puritan brothers, Richard and Joseph Alleine. Ultimately it goes back to the idea of covenant in the Bible.

A covenant is simply an agreement between two (or more) parties. The roots mean "coming together." Treaties between nations, contracts between employees and companies (or between publishers and authors), marriage vows—all are examples of covenants. Covenants can be general or explicit, public or private.

In the Bible, the most important covenants are between God and God's people. Most of them are pretty much "take it or leave it." That is, God says, "I have chosen you to be my people and here's what I will do for you. If you want to accept this offer, here's what you do."

- God blesses Noah and his family and explains that they may eat all the plants and animals of the earth—but no blood. God promises never to flood all the world again. And then God says, "This is the sign of the covenant that I make between me and you and every living creature that is with you, for all future generations: I have set my bow in the clouds, and it shall be a sign of the covenant between me and the earth" (Genesis 9:12–13).

- God calls Abram and promises to make him father of a great nation. Abram accepts the covenant by sacrificing a number of animals and circumcising all the men in his family. And God gives him the new name of Abraham (the name change represents, more or less, a shift in meaning from Big Daddy to Great Daddy) and eventually, a son: Isaac.
- God brings the descendants of Abraham's grandson Israel out of slavery in Egypt and then offers them instructions (in Hebrew, torah) on how to live as God's people.

Near the end of his life, Moses reminds the people of the choice before them: to accept God's choice of them and to live according to God's instruction, or to reject God's instruction and to live as they please—for as long as they can manage without God:

See, I have set before you today life and prosperity, death and adversity. If you obey the commandments of the LORD your God that I am commanding you today, by loving the LORD your God, walking in his ways, and observing his commandments, decrees, and ordinances, then you shall live and become numerous, and the LORD your God will bless you in the land that you are entering to possess. But if your heart turns away and you do not hear, but are led astray to bow down to other gods and serve them, I declare to you today that you shall perish; you shall not live long in the land that you are crossing the Jordan to enter and possess. I call heaven and earth to witness against you today that I have set before you life and death, blessings and curses. Choose life so that you and your descendants may live, loving the LORD your God, obeying him, and holding fast to him; for that means life to you and length of days, so that you may live in the land that the LORD swore to give to your ancestors, to Abraham, to Isaac, and to Jacob. (Deuteronomy 30:15–20)

Much of the rest of the Old Testament is the playing out of this choice, as Israel and Judah repeatedly turn away from God and get themselves into deep trouble, then return to God and prosper. These times of return are often concretized through a national service of covenant renewal.

- On hearing God's warning through the prophet Azariah, King Asa casts out idols, repairs the temple, and leads the people in making a covenant "to seek the LORD, the God of their ancestors, with all their heart and with all their soul" (2 Chronicles 15:12).

- Nearly three centuries later, workers discover a book of God's law while renovating the temple, and King Josiah has it read to all the leaders of Judah. The king makes a personal covenant "to follow the LORD, keeping his commandments, his decrees, and his statutes, with all his heart and all his soul, to perform the words of the covenant that were written in this book" (2 Chronicles 34:31). He then gets all the leaders and all the people of Jerusalem to agree to this covenant renewal.

- After destruction, exile, and return, Ezra brings the book of the law to the struggling returned community. He reads it out (with simultaneous translation, because the people no longer understand Hebrew) and the people rejoice and feast. The leaders study the law for the next three weeks, then assemble the people for a service of covenant renewal including a rehearsal of God's saving action, a time of confession, and a promise to keep the covenant in the future.

In each of these times of renewal, there is no hint that God has ever been unfaithful to the covenant. God's promises are sure, characterized by the word *chesed*, usually translated "steadfast love." Human promises are shaky at best. In the metaphor of the prophet Hosea's life, God is a faithful husband who remains true to his wife despite her infidelities, who keeps trying to bring her back to him. Covenant renewal, then, is a remembering of God's promises and a reaffirmation of human ones. God's reputation as a saving, loving, merciful God is never harmed by our insistence on rushing headlong for our own destruction.

Flash forward two thousand years, past the coming of Christ, the growth of Christianity, the beginnings of the Protestant Reformation. The Reformation emphasis on salvation by grace alone, through faith alone, and the futility of our works to save us, seemed to some to have backfired. They felt that too many people took God's grace for granted: living their lives as "good enough" Christians, going to church on occasion, being no worse than their peers, giving to charity when convenient, and counting on God to make everything come out all right in the end. The idea of following Jesus, seeking to know and do God's will as revealed in his life and teachings, had been forgotten by many.

A Puritan preacher named Richard Alleine was one of many who cried out for a closer following of Christ. How could one claim to be a Christian and yet follow Christ only when convenient? He called for Christians to be do precisely what God commanded, to be "Precisians":

By a Precisian, I mean a sincere circumspect Christian, one whose care and endeavor is to walk uprightly, according to the truth of the gospel, who, withdrawing himself from the fellowship, fashions, and lusts of the world and denying himself the sinful liberties thereof, doth exercise himself to keep a good conscience towards God and men.[1]

Alleine calls on sinners to come back to God, to following God's hard road that leads to life (see Matthew 7:14). Such a return would begin by getting over the threshold of the narrow gate. He recommends five steps for those who want to make such a beginning.

The first step is to establish firmly in one's mind three principles which will help one to continue on the path:

1. That the things which are eternal are unspeakably more considerable than the things which are but temporal.
2. That things not seen are as infallibly certain as the things which are seen.
3. That according to your present choice must be your eternal lot.[2]

The second step is to make your choice and be sure it is a clear choice. A choice for Christ must be a choice against the world and its promises of worldly happiness. Alleine knows that not to choose is, in fact, to choose against Jesus: "If you remain undetermined for Christ, you are determined for the Devil."[3]

The third step is to embark with Christ, to set sail with him as one who has come to rescue you from being marooned with robbers and murderers. As the second step involved renouncing the world, this one involves renouncing one's own righteousness and admitting one's deep sinfulness. Alleine says that sinners can never be received by Christ until they "let go all other props and trust on him alone."[4]

In the fourth step, Alleine calls us to self-abandonment: "Resign and deliver up yourselves to God in Christ."[5] This step includes a thorough description of what such surrender involves, especially in terms of one's work and station. In the midst of this description come two sections that would become parts of the Covenant Prayer:

> Let me come under thy roof, let me be thy servant, and spare not to command me. I will be no longer my own, but give up myself to thy will in all things.[6]
>
> I put myself wholly into thy hands. Put me to what thou wilt, rank me with whom thou wilt. Put me to doing, put me to suffering. Let me be employed for thee or laid aside for thee, exalted for thee or trodden under feet for thee. Let me be full, let me be empty, let me have all things, let me have nothing. I freely and heartily resign all to thy pleasure and disposal.[7]

119

The final step is to "confirm and complete all this by solemn covenant."[8] After explaining what a covenant is, Alleine inserts both instructions and a lengthy covenant prayer. He explains, "Providence hath lately brought to my hand the advice of a dear friend and faithful laborer in the work of the Lord about this matter." In fact, Alleine took the material from a pamphlet by his brother, Joseph, also a Puritan minister. The title was *Directions for a Thorough Conversion to God.* The conclusion of Joseph Alleine's prayer provides the final piece for the Covenant Prayer:

> O dreadful Jehovah, the Lord God omnipotent, Father, Son, and Holy Ghost, thou art now become my covenant friend. And I through thine infinite grace am become thy covenant servant. Amen. So be it. And the covenant which I have made on earth, let it be ratified in Heaven.[9]

I haven't been able to learn when John Wesley first read Alleine's book, published forty years before Wesley's birth. What is certain is Wesley's first reference to using it for a service of covenant renewal. Here is a passage from Wesley's *Journal* entries for August, 1755, when he was in London:

> Wed. 6.—I mentioned to the congregation another means of increasing serious religion, which had been frequently practiced by our forefathers, and

attended with eminent blessing; namely, the joining in a covenant to serve God with all our heart and with all our soul. I explained this for several mornings following; and on Friday many of us kept a fast unto the Lord, beseeching him to give us wisdom and strength, to promise unto the Lord our God and keep it.

Mon. 11.—I explained once more the nature of such an engagement, and the manner of doing it acceptably to God. At six in the evening we met for that purpose, at the French church in Spitalfields. After I had recited the tenor of the covenant pro posed, in the words of that blessed man, Richard Alleine, all the people stood up, in testimony of assent, to the number of about eighteen hundred persons. Such a night I scarce ever saw before. Surely the fruit of it shall remain for ever.[10]

Wesley continued to lead congregations in services of covenant renewal based on Alleine's work for the rest of his life. Many of these were held on the first Sunday of January, though others were held on Christmas or at other times in the year. By 1762, Charles Wesley had written a special hymn for the covenant service. In it he expresses his own theological understanding of covenant renewal.

Come, let us use the grace divine,
And all, with one accord,
In a perpetual cov'nant join
Ourselves to Christ the Lord:
Give up ourselves, through Jesus' power,
His Name to glorify;
And promise, in this sacred hour,
For God to live and die.

The cov'nant we this moment make
Be ever kept in mind;
We will no more our God forsake,
Or cast his words behind.
We never will throw off his fear,
Who hears our solemn vow;
And if thou art well-pleased to hear,
Come down, and meet us now.

Thee, Father, Son, and Holy Ghost,
Let all our hearts receive;
Present with the Celestial host,
The peaceful answer give.
To each the cov'nant blood apply,
Which takes our sins away;
And register our names on high,
And keep us to that day.[11]

Wesley published an abridgment of Alleine's book in his Christian Library. Eventually Alleine's five steps together with his brother's instructions and covenant prayer (as abridged) were reprinted as a pamphlet, *Directions for Renewing our Covenant with God*, which went through thirteen editions between 1780 and 1811.[12] Methodists continued to use Wesley's abridgment of Alleine, more or less intact, for over a century. In 1921, a British Wesleyan Methodist, George B. Robson, published a radically reworked version of the covenant service, cutting much of the material from Alleine and making a full worship service with hymns, prayers, the covenant renewal, and communion. A further revision of this service was printed in 1932, just at the time several British Methodist groups united. This edition contained something very much like the Covenant Prayer as the congregational conclusion to a longer prayer by the minister. The final refinement came in 1936 with *The Book of Offices* of the newly united Methodist Church in England. Robson was one of several members of the subcommittee that worked on the covenant service, and his format was kept. The Covenant Prayer was further shortened.[13] This is the service that was reprinted in the 1964 American *Book of Worship*, whence it finally got to me. (The current United Methodist *Book of Worship*, published in 1992, has returned to including more of Richard Alleine's instructions and Joseph Alleine's prayer as abridged in Wesley's 1780 pamphlet. The Covenant Prayer is in *The United Methodist*

Hymnal—with a couple of inexplicable word changes—as #607, directly following Charles Wesley's covenant hymn.)

So who wrote the Covenant Prayer? Certainly Richard and Joseph Alleine are the ultimate sources for the words. John Wesley gets credit for popularizing their work through the covenant service. George Robson had the idea of creating a short congregational prayer out of pieces from Richard Alleine's directions and Joseph Alleine's prayer. But the final form is truly amazing: something good, short, and to the point created by a committee!

Spiritual Formation

IT'S EASY TO TALK about spiritual formation without ever actually defining the term. That hardly seems fair. So here's a brief introduction to what I mean by spiritual formation. My description is strongly shaped by my studies at the Institute of Formative Spirituality at Duquesne University, where I learned the basics of the Formation Science developed by Fr. Adrian van Kaam and his associates.[1]

Formation is unavoidable. Our whole lives, we are receiving all sorts of input designed to shape how we live and think. Our DNA gives our bodies (and minds, to some extent) a basic shape. Our parents and other early caretakers have a fundamental impact on our development. Teachers, friends, books we read, shows we watch on television (especially commercials), all offer suggestions about who we are and what we should do with our lives. We are constantly bombarded with all kinds of directives. A full stomach urges us to stop eating. A deeply ingrained parental saying asks, "Are you going to be a member of the Clean Plate Club?" A friend says, "Won't you have a little more? I know it's your favorite." We think about our New Year's resolution, our project to lose weight this year.

Maybe we remember a doctor's chiding, "If you don't lower that cholesterol, you're heading for a heart attack." And we have to decide how we'll respond to these contradictory directives. The decision might reshape our bodies, the course of the evening, our relationship with our friend, our health, the length of our lives. It will reinforce some directives and dampen others, forming or reforming habits. At every moment we are being formed by and giving form to the world around us.

This ability to make decisions about our own formation is an important part of what it means to be human. We can choose to rise above the various directives that have shaped us in the past, to transcend the givens of our lives. As humans we continue to believe that we can make choices, even if only in our attitude toward circumstances where we have no control—a terminal illness, a natural disaster, a concentration camp.

Another distinctive part of human formation is our ability to step back from the process and examine our choices and our way of choosing. In the example above, we probably wouldn't take the time at the table to list all the conflicting directives, evaluate them, and come to a conscious decision. It is much more likely that most or even all of the decision making is subconscious, as we follow the deep ruts of old habits. But later that night, as we reach for the antacid and wonder why on earth we took a second piece of cheesecake, we may stop and bring the implicit decision-making process into the light of consciousness.

Looking carefully at how we came to one decision can tell us a lot about ourselves, our habits, our priorities, our dreams. Looking at different areas or spheres of our lives may help us list all of the directives at play. One sphere is what we would usually call ourselves— our aspirations and inspirations, our thoughts and emotions, our bodily feelings, our habits and memories. Another is the sphere of interpersonal relations— friends who speak to us directly, authors who speak through their books. A third sphere is the world we know directly, the situation in which we live and work, the groups we are part of. Finally there is the world we know only indirectly, through television, radio, newspapers, magazines, and so forth. Each of these spheres can be a source of directives that contribute to every decision. So blaming my parents' insistence on a clean plate for my overeating ignores all the other contributing factors of my own sweet tooth, my friend's insistence that I should eat more, my situation (I'm a pastor and gluttony is the only "deadly sin" winked at by congregations), or the call to waste nothing when others are starving around the world.

There is one more source of directives, and a most important one. Under or behind each of the spheres is the mysterious presence of God, calling, offering guidance. God's unique call to each of us is the heart of who we most deeply are. God reaches out to us directly through the Holy Spirit's presence in our lives, whether as a small voice heard only in the quiet of prayer, a deep gut feeling we can't dismiss, or a rushing wind that drives us in a certain direction. God speaks to us indirectly through the people, things, and events in our lives; through friends, spiritual writers, the liturgy of worship; through music, paintings, and other arts. God speaks to us as we read Scripture, sometimes through, sometimes in spite of the words on the page. When we pay attention to these divine directives, then we become aware that our formation is truly spiritual formation.

If our formation is guided by God, then it has a direction, a goal. That goal is the reforming and transforming of our lives (with the help of divine grace) to become more and more in tune with God's call to us. Van Kaam calls this goal consonance, from Latin roots meaning "sounding together." When my guitar is in tune, then picking the low E string will cause the high E string to vibrate, to sound together with the low note. The high B string also vibrates because it is in harmony with the low E. When our lives are consonant, we are in harmony with ourselves, with God, with what is best in the world around us, with what is holy.

In the Old Testament, the concept of *shalom* is a reasonable equivalent to consonance. *Shalom* is not just peace as the absence of conflict. It is when all is right with the world, when things are the way God meant them to be. In the New Testament, the Kingdom or Reign of God, life in Christ, and the call to unconditional love are ways of talking about consonance. Later Christian writers have spoken of the imitation of Christ or (particularly among Methodists) of going on to perfection.

So far I have spoken of formation directives as if they were discrete bits of guidance, coming at us almost at random. This is not really the case. There exist complex structures of interrelated directives that support one another and sketch more or less complete pictures of the sort of person they would form if one followed the whole structure. These structures are formation traditions. Some of these structures are vast and all-inclusive, such as the formation traditions of the great religions. They offer guidance for all of life from birth to death, with many variations for different circumstances and callings. From the tradition we learn how to welcome a baby, how to raise a child, what things are important to learn, how to court and marry, how to work and what kinds of work are suitable, how to live in community, how to worship, how to treat the aged, what to do when someone dies. Other formation traditions are much less inclusive and deal only with selected aspects of life. These include such formation traditions as the Boy Scouts, Alcoholics Anonymous, the Marine Corps, the "company way" for the employees of a business, or "how we've always done it in our family." But all formation traditions contain many linked directives that reinforce one another.

Formation traditions have a variety of ways to teach and reinforce their way of life—their structure of directives—in followers. One of the most important is through writings (sometimes regarded as sacred) such as the Bible, the Qur'an, the Big Blue Book of AA, or the Little Red Book of Maoist Communism. Indoctrination (bringing people into the teaching of the tradition) also uses ritual, songs, proverbs, art, creeds, group work, mentoring, and many other means. In the United States, we learn the formation tradition of All-American Individualism through the Pledge of Allegiance in school, flag ceremonies at camp or at military or police funerals, singing "The Star Spangled Banner" at sporting events, fireworks and the cannon blasts of "The 1812 Overture" on the Fourth of July, reading the Gettysburg Address on Memorial Day, Pilgrim and Indian pageants at Thanksgiving, movies with tough, loner heroes played by John Wayne or Clint Eastwood or Steven Segal, and the great childhood heroes: Superman, the Lone Ranger, and Popeye (at least, when I was a child—there are others now). Large formation traditions often contain subtraditions with their own special formation sources. Episcopalians have *The Book of Common Prayer*; Methodists, the journal and sermons of John Wesley and the hymns of his brother Charles; Presbyterians, the Westminster Confession and other creedal formulations. But all are part of the larger Christian formation tradition.

Becoming part of a formation tradition means accepting these directives as a package. Of course, most of us find ourselves aligned with multiple traditions. Inevitably we are faced with contradictory directives. Do we blast the bad guys with Clint or love our enemies as Jesus commanded? Is blood thicker than water, or is gang loyalty more important than family? The answer usually indicates that we have somehow ranked our various formation traditions, assigning different priorities to each. The directives of our most cherished tradition will outrank directives from another source. One can picture the various traditions stacked in a sort of step pyramid, with less attention given to the smaller steps near the top and ultimate authority vested in the base. That is, faced with a choice, we give greatest weight to our foundational tradition. If it offers no clear directive, we may go on to the next tradition for guidance, and so on up the steps. This means that traditions near the bottom tend to be more nearly all-inclusive, while upper traditions may give very explicit guidance in particular areas. How we stack the pyramid determines whether, for instance, we are American Christians (where the American tradition comes first) or are Christians who are also patriotic Americans (as long as love of country doesn't conflict with love of Christ). One aspect of deep conversion—

as opposed to just joining a new group—is that the new group's tradition becomes the foundation of our personal pyramid. Being a Christian, following Christ, becomes more important than anything else. Or, all the world is seen in the light of the Twelve Steps and Twelve Traditions of Alcoholics Anonymous. Or, we analyze every aspect or our lives in light of Carl Jung's writings. Such conversions can cause great upheavals in our lives.

Our formation is not a smooth upward slope, every day getting better and better, growing more consonant. We grow by fits and starts. Sometimes we grow toward greater consonance, sometimes away from it. Throughout our lives we can point to key events, moments of crisis. Though the crises may be very different in content, they tend to follow a basic structure or plot.

The plot begins in stability. During a relatively settled part of our life, we come to a basic pattern of being and doing. Usually it represents a working compromise between the various directives striving to form our lives. The pattern will certainly include contradictions, dissonances. We have come to a way of damping down the clash so we can ignore it. I diet at home and overeat in restaurants. I order salads in restaurants and go home to eat a pint of Ben and Jerry's "Chubby Hubby" (something cannibalistic about that). I fast during the week and feast on

Sundays. All of these are possible compromises between contradictory directives.

Then something happens. A new directive breaks in and exposes the dissonance inherent in our lives. What may begin as a small crack soon becomes shattering. The basic pattern suddenly will not hold together. We recognize that what had seemed like small surface contradictions mask deep conflicts between established habits and basic directives in our foundational tradition or in our deepest sense of who we are and who God calls us to be.

In the midst of crisis, we begin to look seriously at ourselves, perhaps with the help of others. We come to new decisions, attempt to form new habits. We may make radical changes, reordering our tradition pyramid or rejecting long-established patterns of living. More often, though, the change is small. Slowly we form a new, slightly more consonant, "working self." Van Kaam calls this working self a current life form—the shape our lives take for a while, but not forever.

Note that this increase in consonance may be internal consistency or greater conformation to the world around us, not necessarily a move toward greater consonance with God and God's call to us. That's why it's helpful, especially in times of crisis, to discuss our decisions with someone (or a group) who can help us examine our choice in the light of Christ.

This movement from one way of living—one current life form—through a time of crisis and ensuing chaos to a new (slightly revised) current life form is the basic plot of our lives. We may see it reflected in the Exodus story as the children of Israel move from a settled but oppressed life as slaves in Egypt to a long time of wandering and reformation in the desert to a new settled life in the Promised Land. The bad news is that we can't get from Egypt to the Promised Land without going through the desert. The good news is that, with God's help, we can reach the Promised Land. The sad news is that we can easily make the Promised Land into a new Egypt from which we must again be set free. The cycle continues. Old Testament scholar Walter Brueggeman speaks of this plot as the movement from "being securely oriented" through "being painfully disoriented" to "being surprisingly reoriented"—surprising because it is, at least in part, the working of God's grace that brings us to the new orientation.[2]

The concepts I've presented here—directives, the formation field, the persistence of the idea that we can make some formation choices in any situation, the importance of formation traditions, and the basic plot of ongoing formation—provide a structure for looking at our lives. Spiritual direction, whether individually or in a group, is the process of paying attention to how our spirits are being formed and how God is calling us in the midst of our formation. It is seeking actively to make our lives more consonant, to abandon ourselves to God's guidance.

Endnotes

INTRODUCTION

1 Keith Miller, *The Taste of New Wine* (Brewster, Massachusetts: Paraclete Press, 1965, 1991, 1992), 33.

2 Ernest J. Gaines, *A Lesson Before Dying* (New York: Vintage Books, 1993), 97.

3 *The Book of Worship for Church and Home* (Nashville: The United Methodist Publishing House, 1964), 387.

4 Garrison Keillor, *Woebegon Boy* (New York: Viking, 1997), 135f.

5 Teresa of Avila, *The Way of Perfection*, edited by Henry L. Carrigan, Jr., (Brewster, Massachusetts: Paraclete Press, 2000), 108.

6 Ibid., 107.

CHAPTER 1: SURRENDER

1 William Ernest Henley, "Invictus" (p.d.).

2 Adrian van Kaam and Susan Muto, *Formation Guide for Becoming Spiritually Mature* (Pittsburgh: Epiphany Association, 1991), 36.

3 Richard Alleine, *Vindiciae Pietatis: or, A Vindication of Godliness in the Greatest Strictness and Spirituality of It from the Imputations of Folly and Fancy. Together with Several Directions for the Attaining and Maintaining of a Godly Life* (London: n.p., 1663), 214f. In this and other quotes from Alleine, spelling and punctuation have been modernized.

4 Hannah Whitall Smith, *The Christian's Secret of a Happy Life* (New York: Ballantine Books, 1986), 22f.

5 Ignatius of Loyola, *The Spiritual Exercises*, paragraph 234, translated by George E. Ganss, S.J., in *Ignatius of Loyola: Spiritual Exercises and Selected Works*, edited by George E. Ganss, S.J. (New York: Paulist Press, 1991), 177.

6 John Foley, S.J., "Take, Lord, Receive" in *Glory and Praise* (Phoenix: North American Liturgy Resouces, 1977), 136.

7 John of the Cross, *The Ascent of Mount Carmel*, Book 2, Chapter 5, Section 7 in *The Collected Works of Saint John of the Cross*, translated by Kieran Kavanaugh, O.C.D., and Otilio Rodriquez, O.C.D. (Washington: ICS Publications, 1991), 165.

8 Irenaeus, *Against Heresies*, Book 4, Chapter 20, Section 7, translated by Alexander Roberts and James Donaldson in *The Ante-Nicene Fathers,* Volume 1, (Albany, Oregon: AGES Software, 1997), 973.

CHAPTER 2: GOD'S CALL

1 Alleine, 211f.

2 Alleine, 215.

3 Jean-Pierre de Caussade, *Abandonment to Divine Providence*, trans. By John Beevers (Garden City, NY: Image Books, 1975), 83.

4 Ibid., 61.

CHAPTER 3: ACCEPTANCE

1 Thomas Merton, *The Sign of Jonas* (Garden City, NY: Image Books, 1956), 202f.

2 Dylan Thomas, "Do Not Go Gentle into That Good Night" in *The Pocket Book of Modern Verse*, edited by Oscar Williams (New York: Washington Square Press, 1972), 486.

3 John Yungblut, *On Hallowing One's Diminishments* (Wallingford, PA: Pendle Hill Publications, 1990), 6.

4 Ibid.

5 Pierre Teilhard de Chardin, *The Divine Milieu* (New York: Harper Torchbooks, 1968), 89f.

6 Thomas H. Green, S.J., *When the Well Runs Dry: Prayer Beyond the Beginnings* (Notre Dame, IN: Ave Maria Press, 1979), 143.

7 Ibid., 144.

8 Ibid.

CHAPTER 4: LAID ASIDE

1 Carlo Carretto, *Letters from the Desert* (Maryknoll, NY: Orbis Books, 1972), 14.

2 Ibid., 16.

3 Ron DelBene has worked extensively with teaching breath prayer to people who are terminally ill. He wrote of these experiences (with help from Mary and Herb Montgomery) in *Into the Light: A Simple Way to Pray with the Sick and the Dying* (Nashville: Upper Room Books, 1988).

4 Isaac Watts, "I'll Praise My Maker While I've Breath" in *The United Methodist Hymnal*, (Nashville: The United Methodist Publishing House, 1989), #60.

CHAPTER 5: STATUS

1 Thérèse de Lisieux, *The Story of a Soul: The Autobiography of Saint Thérèse of Lisieux*, translated by Michael Day (Rockford, IL: Tan Books and Publishers, Inc., 1997), 97f.

2 If you did not immediately think of *The Velveteen Rabbit* by Margery Williams, then go find a copy and read it now.

3 *The Story of a Soul*, 2.

4 Teresa of Avila, *The Interior Castle,* in *The Collected Works of St. Teresa of Avila*, Volume 2, Sixth Dwelling Places, Chapter 10, translated by Otilio Rodriguez, O.C.D., and Kieran Kavanaugh, O.C.D. (Washington: ICS Publications, 1980), 420f.

CHAPTER 6: EMPTINESS

1 Daniel Iverson, "Spirit of the Living God" in *The United Methodist Hymnal*, #393.

2 Edwin Hatch, "Breathe on Me, Breath of God" in *The United Methodist Hymnal*, #420.

3 Charles Wesley, "Jesus, Thine All-Victorious Love" in *The United Methodist Hymnal*, #422.

4 John of the Cross, *The Dark Night*, in *Collected Works*, 399 (Book 2, Chapter 3, Paragraph 3).

5 Ibid., 404 (Bk. 2, Ch. 6, Par. 2).

6 Ibid., 429 (Bk. 2, Ch. 14, Par. 3)

7 Green, 146.

CHAPTER 7: ADDICTION

1 Morton T. Kelsey, *The Other Side of Silence: A Guide to Christian Meditation* (New York: Paulist Press, 1976), 243.

2 John of the Cross discusses this night in *The Ascent of Mount Carmel.*

CHAPTER 8: YIELDING EVERYTHING

1 Adrian van Kaam, *Fundamental Formation,* Formative Spirituality, Vol. 1 (New York: Crossroad, 1989), 221.

2 Caussade, 74f.

3 John H. Sammis, "Trust and Obey" in *The United Methodist Hymnal*, #467.

4 Hannah Hurnard, *Hinds' Feet on High Places* (Wheaton, IL: Tyndale House Publishers, Inc., 1977), 84.

5 Ibid., 211.

6 John Wesley, "The Use of Money" (Sermon 50), in *The Works of John Wesley*, Volume 6 (Albany, Oregon: AGES Software, 1997), 148f.

7 Bernard of Clairvaux, "On Loving God" in *Bernard of Clairvaux: Selected Works*, translated by Gillian R. Evans (New York: Paulist Press, 1987), 189.

8 "My God, I Love Thee" translated from anonymous Latin by Edward Caswall in *The United Methodist Hymnal*, #470.

9 Hurnard, 214.

10 Bernard, 196.

11 Ibid.

12 Ibid., 200f.

13 Ibid., 101.

14 Alleine, 156–158.

CHAPTER 9: IN CONCLUSION

1 The Didache 8:2 in *The New Testament and Other Early Christian Writings: A Reader,* edited by Bart D. Ehrman (New York: Oxford University Press, 1998), 315.

2 "Westminster Shorter Catechism" in *Creeds of the Church* (Albany, Oregon: AGES Software, 1997), 92.

3 Joseph Alleine is the brother of Richard Alleine, who quoted a covenant prayer by Joseph in his book. Just this portion of the Covenant Prayer is taken from Joseph's prayer. For the full story, see Appendix A.

4 John of the Cross, "The Dark Night" stanzas 5 and 6 in *Collected Works*, 51.

5 Bernard, "On Loving God," 191.

APPENDIX A

1 Alleine, 4.

2 Ibid., 195f.

3 Ibid., 204.

4 Ibid., 208.

5 Ibid., 210.

6 Ibid., 213.

7 Ibid., 214.

8 Ibid., 215.

9 Ibid., 224.

10 John Wesley, *The Complete Works of John Wesley, Volume 2: Journals 1745–1760*, (Albany, Oregon: AGES Software, 1997), 382f.

11 Charles Wesley, "Come Let Us Use the Grace Divine" in *The United Methodist Hymnal*, #606.

12 The history from pamphlet to the creation of the Covenant Prayer is based on *The Renewal of the Covenant in the Methodist Tradition* by David Tripp (London: Epworth Press, 1969). The information about the pamphlet is from pages 56 and 57.

13 See Tripp, 73–78 and 104–107.

APPENDIX B

1 Adrian van Kaam's Formation Science (more formally The Science of Foundational Human Formation) is described most completely in his seven-volume series *Formative Spirituality*, published by Crossroads. *The Transcendent Self*, published by Epiphany Press, offers a more accessible introduction to the subject.

2 Walter Brueggemann, *Praying the Psalms* (Winona, Minnesota: Saint Mary's Press, 1993), 14.

Do you know of other people who would enjoy this book?
Share it with them!

To order individual copies of the book, call 1-800-451-5006.

Most Paraclete books are available at special quantity discounts for bulk purchases for churches, hospitals, hospices, libraries, and schools. For more information on bulk purchases, call 1-800-451-5006.

For more information or to order other Paraclete books, visit www.paracletepress.com

Surrendering to God
1-55725-284-X $13.95

ORDER FORM FOR CONSUMERS ONLY (1–5 COPIES)

Payable in US funds only. Book price: $13.95 each copy. Postage & handling: $6.50 (1–2 books); $6.95 (3 books); $7.95 (4-5 books). MA residents add 5% sales tax. We accept Visa, MC, or checks. Call (800) 451-5006, fax (508) 255-5705, or mail your orders to:

PARACLETE PRESS
PO Box 1568
Orleans, MA 02653

BILL TO: _____

Address _____

City_____ ST _____ ZIP _____

Daytime phone#_____

SHIP TO: _____

Address _____

City _____ ST _____ ZIP _____

BILL MY

Credit card #_____ exp. _____

❑ Visa   ❑ MC

Signature_____

Please allow 2 weeks for US delivery. This offer is subject to change without notice. Tracking code: MSTG	Book Total: _____
	Applicable Sales Tax: _____
	Postage & Handling: _____
	Total Amount Due: _____